LOVE UNDER CAPRICORN

"That gives us plenty of time then," said Mark, and he drew Jo into his arms. They kissed, and Jo felt all the things she'd felt the first time — her heart fluttering, her pulse quickening. And above all, it felt so easy with Mark, so right.

TENDER ◆ HEARTS

Love Under Capricorn

by
BRENDA APSLEY

WORLD INTERNATIONAL PUBLISHING LIMITED
MANCHESTER

World International books
in the TENDER HEARTS series

Take Two
Love Match
Making Waves
Say It With Flowers
Midsummer Madness
Love Under Capricorn
This Heart is not for Hire
A Time To Choose
Loving and Losing
Can't Fight Love
Tide of Love
Flatmates
Taking Sides
Oceans Apart
Season of Love
He Stole Her Heart
Her Banned Boyfriend
Her Whirlwind Romance
Caught Between the Two
When Friends Fall Out
Just Good Friends
Island of Dreams
Heart Beat
Our Song

CHAPTER ONE

NEW GIRLS

The two girls walked uncertainly around the small, impersonal room, carefully avoiding the two new suitcases and carrier bags piled in the middle of a square of carpet. They carefully avoided looking at each other, too, heads lowered. Both felt new, unsure, a little embarrassed. When they both stretched out a hand to open the wardrobe door, their hands touched, and they both drew away quickly.

"Sorry."

"Sorry. I was just . . ."

The door opened and a tall, dark woman walked in. She carried a clipboard and looked up from the list pinned to it to the number on the door – four – and back again. "So, you got here on time," she said briskly. "Have a good journey?" But she didn't wait for an answer. "Have you introduced yourselves?"

"No, we, er . . . we . . ."

"I see." She read from her list. "Josephine Carr and Lynn Brooking, yes? Which is which?"

The taller of the two girls spoke first. "I'm Josephine — Jo — Carr."

The woman didn't wait for the other girl to speak. "So — Josephine, meet Lynn."

The girls looked uncertainly at each other. A pink flush crept up Lynn's neck. "Hello," she said, extending her hand uncertainly.

Jo took it, and laughed. "Seems so formal, doesn't it?" she said. "Like a sort of ritual, a . . ."

The woman interrupted her. "And I'm Elaine McNeil, Nurse Tutor. Come on, I'll show you the kitchen and lounge."

She led the way along a pale green-painted corridor — hospital green, Jo thought, typical — and into a small kitchen. "You share with ten others on this corridor." She flung open a door into an adjoining room. "The lounge is in there." She picked up a half-full coffee mug and put it into the sink. "This is communal living, and we expect you all to keep the place clean and tidy. You've no mums to run around after you here."

"What about cooking, er, Elaine?" said Jo, glancing at the cooker.

"Most foundation nurses just use the kitchen for snacks and drinks. Remember, you'll have most of your meals in the canteen. I'll take you there later. And I'm *Miss* McNeil."

The emphasis was very definitely on the Miss, and Jo almost winced. "Sorry, er, *Miss* McNeil." She emphasised the word 'Miss'.

Miss McNeil tucked the clipboard under her arm and led the way back to the girls' room. "I'll leave you to unpack now," she said. "Oh, I almost forgot –" pointing to two parcels on one of the beds. "You'll find your uniforms in there. Try them on and let me know if there are any problems." She paused at the door as the two girls looked uncertainly at the parcels, then laughed (a rather forced laugh, Jo thought) and said, "Go on – they won't bite!"

But *you* might, thought Jo, as she looked for her name on one of the labels. She ripped off the paper and shook out three pale blue dresses. "Not exactly high fashion, are they?" she said, holding one of the dresses against herself and looking in the mirror. "And the shoes we have to wear! Aren't they hideous?"

Lynn had unpacked her uniform and was hanging the dresses in the wardrobe, smoothing out the creases. "I don't think they're supposed to be fashionable, just practical," she said. "Nursing's hard work. I don't want to wear stilettos all day."

Jo rolled her eyes to the ceiling with a 'sorry I spoke' look. She took a small white cap from the parcel and perched it on top of her head. She looked in the mirror. "Well, I suppose I'll soon look like a nurse, but I certainly don't feel like one. Do you?"

"No, not yet," Lynn said slowly. "I think I'll really feel like a nurse when we go on the wards. I can't wait."

Jo wasn't quite so sure. She shrugged. "Oh, well, I suppose we'd better unpack before Miss McNeil comes back." She mimicked the nurse tutor's soft Scots accent. "This is communal living, and we must keep the place clean and tidy. Which bed do you want?"

Lynn was busy laying sweaters in a drawer. "I don't mind; you choose," she said over her shoulder.

Jo glanced around the room. "I'll have the one nearest the washbasin," she said. "Then I won't have so far to crawl in the mornings. I hate getting up early, don't you? I'm dreading shifts. Imagine having to be on duty at seven in the morning."

"I don't mind getting up early," said Lynn. "And look, this'll help."

She took a huge Mickey Mouse alarm clock from her case and put it on her bedside table. "This will wake us up on time – guaranteed."

Jo grimaced. She hated mornings, loud mornings in particular. She was used to hearing her brother's radio blaring away from seven o'clock, but that was at a reasonable distance, and Jo could blot out the sound quite successfully by putting a pillow over her head. She preferred a quiet start to the day, a gentle shake from her mum and a mug of coffee delivered to her bedside.

Jo thought wistfully of home. That's all in the past now, she told herself sternly. From now on you're on your own, Jo Carr. She stood up again and started to unpack. And you'd better make the best of it. You're eighteen now, living away from home, an adult. And soon you'll be a nurse. Nurse Jo Carr. It sounded odd.

Lynn had finished her unpacking and had stowed her suitcase under the bed while Jo was still gazing around, deciding where to put her old teddy and her moth-eaten panda. Jo caught Lynn looking curiously at them, and felt a bit embarrassed. "Mum made me pack them," she said unconvincingly. "She thought they might help if I got homesick. You know what parents are like."

"Mmm," said Lynn. "I'm going to make a coffee. Would you like one?"

"Please," Jo answered over her shoulder, trying to cram a big sweater into an already full drawer.

"There! Finished at last!" said Jo triumphantly as Lynn came back to the room with two mugs of steaming coffee. "It's beginning to look more like home already."

Not my home, thought Lynn, as she looked around the room. Jo's shoes lay in a heap by the open wardrobe door, two piles of paperbacks wobbled unsteadily under the coffee table, and scarves and long rows of beads and a thick leather belt were draped from the anglepoise lamp at the desk. Hairbrushes and bottles of shampoo spilled off the narrow shelf over the wash basin, and two odd socks and a bundle of knickers decorated the top of the chest of drawers.

Jo caught Lynn's disapproving look and grabbed her coffee. "Don't worry about those – I'll find a home for them later."

Jo threw herself onto her bed and pushed her hand into a large canvas bag. She called it a handbag, but it was more of a rucksack. "Got it," she said after searching around inside for a few minutes, and pulled out a crumpled magazine. She flicked to the back pages then settled herself against the pillows. She read silently for a few seconds, then said, "You can say that again," and threw the magazine aside.

"Say what again?" asked Lynn.

Jo nodded towards the magazine. "My horo-scope," she said. "I'm a Capricorn. It says I'm going to go on a journey – which I have – and that I'm going to meet a tall, dark stranger. Dead right, eh?"

Lynn looked puzzled. "Yes, I can see the journey bit, but the tall, dark stranger? Not me, surely? It's stretching the imagination a bit to describe me as tall and dark."

Jo laughed. "Not you, stupid – Miss McNeil, of course."

Lynn laughed too. "Aaah."

"They're usually right, you know," said Jo, staring up at the ceiling.

"What are?"

"Horoscopes. Astrologers. The stars. I must get a newspaper tomorrow morning to see what's in store for us." She picked up the magazine again. "What star sign are you?"

Lynn hesitated. "Virgo, I think."

"You think?" said Jo, incredulously. "Don't you know? When's your birthday?"

"Tenth of September."

"Yes, that's Virgo," said Jo. She began to read from the magazine. "It says a rough patch is coming to an end, that there's light at the end of the tunnel for you. And you may meet a new romantic partner. Oh, and the colour white is going to be significant."

"What rubbish," said Lynn, gazing out of the window into the hospital grounds. "Surely you don't believe that stuff? It's ridiculous. How can all the people born at a certain time have the same things happening to them?"

"Ah, it's all down to interpretation," Jo said calmly. She'd met criticism like this before, and was practised at answering it. "You may not think this makes sense now, but it will, I promise you it will. Wait and see."

Lynn shook her head. "I haven't had a rough patch to come out of, I'm not looking for a romance, and I don't see how white can be significant. Now if it had said blue I might have taken some notice, what with our new uniforms and all, but . . ."

Jo waved her arm in front of Lynn's face. "Okay, okay, call it nonsense if you like, but I'll prove you wrong. Just wait and see."

Jo and Lynn got to know quite a bit about each other over the next few hours, and Jo began to wonder how they'd ever live together in that one small room. Chalk and cheese was almost an understatement. Jo knew that she was untidy and disorganized, but she certainly didn't intend to change — why should she? If Lynn wanted to be neat and tidy, well, she'd have to be neat and tidy in her part of the room, wouldn't she? And leave Jo to do her own thing.

Jo watched Lynn as she moved around the room, dressed in her neat, *broderie anglaise* nightdress, rearranging books and papers, moving the fruit bowl until it was right in the centre of a shelf, and squaring up two magazines. Typical Virgo. Jo, sprawled on her bed, comfortable in her *Snoopy* night-shirt, with a reassuring clutter of clothes, books, handbag and papers around her – not to mention the teddy and the panda – couldn't help staring.

Lynn suddenly became aware that Jo was staring at her, and looked up. "What is it?" she asked.

Jo was taken by surprise, and, as she often did, spoke without thinking, putting into words exactly what was in her head. "Why did you decide to be a nurse?" she said, and didn't wait for an answer. "I mean, you seem so particular, so neat and tidy. Surely nursing is too . . ." she searched for just the right word, ". . . too plain *messy* for someone like you? It's not all soothing fevered brows and making neat hospital corners on the beds, you know – nursing can be a dirty, smelly job."

Lynn flushed, and put down the books she was handling. "I know that," she said. "I've been to interviews just like you, you know. I know it's not all roses. But it's what I want to do; it's what I'm going to do. And I'm going to be good at it."

"Okay, okay, sorry I spoke," said Jo.

But Lynn hadn't finished. "And what gives

you the right to criticize me? What's wrong with being neat and tidy? It's not a crime, is it?"

"No, it's just that you seem, well, obsessed, almost," said Jo, surprised at Lynn's reaction.

"And you seem, well, a slob, almost," said Lynn coldly. "I'm going to bed. Goodnight," she added.

Jo was stunned. The mouse had turned into a lion — and a fierce lion, at that. Well, well, this was going to be interesting, if nothing else.

"Goodnight," Jo said a few seconds later, and turned out the light.

CHAPTER TWO

REVELATIONS

It was Friday evening, and Jo put her coffee mug in front of her on the formica table in the kitchen. She ripped off her cap and threw it down in front of her. "Phew, am I glad that's over. One week, five days – yet we seem to have crammed an awful lot in, don't you think, Nishma?"

Nishma's face wore a 'maybe' look. "But I knew it was going to be hard work," she said. "My mum's a nurse, remember. And I think training now is much better than when she was a student. It was all standing to attention when Matron passed – and it was months before you got your hands on a patient."

Jo laughed. "Well, the only patient we've handled wasn't exactly in the best of health, was he? Lynn and I were so nervous lifting that dummy from the bed. I'm sure we'd have dropped a real, live patient."

"I doubt it."

Jo stared into her coffee. "Big Mac certainly didn't seem to rate our performance."

"Big Mac? Who do you mean?" asked Nishma.

"Big Mac," said Jo. "You know, the McNeil of McNeil — St Stephen's answer to Miss Jean Brodie."

Nishma smiled. "You shouldn't say that. And I don't think Miss McNeil's so bad."

Jo put on a strong Scots accent. She sounded like Muriel Gray. "And she's no so good, either," she said. "She's all starch and straight caps and sensible shoes. She's not what I think of when I think of a nurse."

"And what do you think of when you think of a nurse?"

"Oh, someone warm, and caring — and capable, and . . ."

Nishma put an imaginary violin to her shoulder and started to play. "That's all a bit hearts and flowers, isn't it? Nurses in Mills and Boon doctor-nurse romance stories might be like that, but it's not very realistic, is it?" She paused. "And I thought you'd told Lynn that nursing was often dirty, smelly — messy?"

Jo looked up quickly. "Did she tell you I said that?"

"I didn't read it in my horoscope." Nishma laughed. "Yes, she told me what you'd said. I think you were a bit hard on her. She can't help being the way she is, any more than any of us can. So she's very neat and tidy. So what?"

Jo tipped her chair back and balanced it on two legs. "But you don't have to live with her. With Lynn it's a case of 'a place for everything and everything in its place'. Honestly, I think she'll tidy me away, one of these days."

"You're exaggerating of course. She can't be that bad."

"She is. She is, believe me. Did you pack dusters to bring with you? Did you? It's ridiculous. And anyway, I like living like a slob. I think there are better things to do than dust and tidy and wash and clean."

"That's probably because your mum did it all at home."

"I suppose so. But it's not normal, is it, Nishma? Lynn's so uptight, so – oh, I don't know – so rigid. Everything's got to be done by the book."

Nishma glanced into the lounge. "Where is Lynn, anyway?"

"Oh, she'll be washing the windows, or ironing the curtains or something."

"Come on."

"Okay. I think she said something about washing her hair," said Jo. "Then – would you believe – she's going to go through this week's notes. Then it'll be lights out at ten on the dot."

Nishma paused, as if wondering if she should speak or not. "You know, I think you're being a bit hard on Lynn. I don't think she's very happy."

"How could she be, stuck in her room all the time?"

"No, I don't mean that. It's something she said the other day. About her family. I think she was very unhappy at home, under a lot of pressure. I feel sorry for her."

Jo scraped her chair back and put her coffee mug in the sink. "Well I don't." She opened the door. "See you later." She looked back over her shoulder and fluttered her eyelashes at Nishma. "I'm going to slip into something a little more comfortable."

Jo pushed open the door of her room. "Lynn, have you seen my . . ."

She stopped in mid-stride and stared at the desk. Lynn was sitting with her head in her arms, her body racked by huge sobs.

"What's the matter?" said Jo. "Are you ill? Shall I get someone?"

Lynn didn't answer; but neither did the sobs subside.

Jo went over and put her hand on Lynn's shoulder. "What's the matter?" she asked quietly. "Can I help? Do you want to talk about it?"

Lynn raised a tear-stained face, red and puffy. Jo thought she'd never seen anyone look so miserable in all her life. And she'd never felt so useless in all her life. What could she do? What could she say?

Lynn blew her nose and looked up at Jo. "Sorry," she said – and the sobs started again. "Sorry – I'll be – alright – just . . ."

Jo looked around the room for some sort of inspiration. "Would a drink of water help? Shall I get one? Or a cup of tea?"

Lynn nodded her head and blew her nose again. The sobs were smaller now. "Yes, water, please."

Jo rushed into the kitchen and turned on the cold tap. "What's the matter?" asked Nishma, looking up from her magazine. "You look white as a sheet."

Jo was almost out of the door, glass in hand. "Oh, it's . . ." then she stopped, shrugged her shoulders, and gave Nishma a 'don't ask' look.

When she got back to her room, Lynn looked calmer. She looked up, took a drink, then said, "Sorry."

"Stop saying that," said Jo. "It's okay. Don't worry about it." She paused. "Would it help to talk about it? I'm not what you'd call a really great listener, but I'll try."

Lynn smiled a small, weak smile. "Oh, you'll think I'm being silly."

Jo pulled up a chair close to Lynn's. "No I

won't. Come on, talk to me. Tell me what's wrong."

"It's nothing . . . it's just . . ."

"It isn't nothing," said Jo firmly. "You don't get upset like that about nothing. Come on — it'll help if you tell me."

Lynn took a deep breath and stared at her hands, which twisted a handkerchief in her lap. "I'm frightened," she said quietly, "I don't know if I can get through the training. I'm afraid I'll fail the exams, the practical, the . . ."

"But we're all feeling a bit like that," said Jo. "I don't know if I'll make it, either, and neither do all the others. But it's early days."

"But I have to make a success of this. I have to," said Lynn, wiping her red eyes. "I must do well. Average won't be good enough. I . . ."

Jo interrupted her. "What do you mean? Who says average isn't good enough? I'll be pleased if I get average marks, I can tell you. And you work hard, you're really conscientious."

"I have to work hard," said Lynn. "It doesn't come easy. And it's my parents. They expect such a lot of me. I can't let them down — I just can't."

"But you can only do your best," said Jo.

Lynn sighed. "You don't understand. You see, my parents are both doctors. Mum's a surgeon and Dad's a GP. It was always accepted that I'd be a doctor, too. But my A level grades weren't good enough. I worked really hard, honestly, Jo, but I just couldn't do any better. I've got to get through this course, do well, or I'll just die. They're disappointed with me already."

Jo thought momentarily of her family, her home: warm, supportive, happy, and felt a pang of real pity for Lynn. "But you've done well already, getting on the course. Not everyone who applied was accepted, you know, not by a long way."

"I know," said Lynn. "But my parents – they're so successful, so able, so capable. They can't understand how I turned out so – thick. I didn't inherit their intelligence – I didn't even inherit their good looks. I'm the ugly duckling of the family. That's what they call me – and Mum says she doesn't think I'll ever turn into a beautiful swan, like in the story."

Jo was horrified. "What? Your mother said that? Surely it was a joke?"

"No, no joke. You see, it's all so easy for them. Everything they do turns out right. I just don't think they can understand that I'm not clever like them, that for me even getting here was hard work. That's why I've got to get this training right."

"So they'll be proud of you?" asked Jo, thinking of her own mum, who'd be proud of her kids even if they had green hair and their heads on upside down.

Lynn laughed a small, bitter laugh. "Oh, there's no chance of that," she said. "They'll never be proud of having a daughter as a mere nurse when they expected me to become a top doctor. No, the best I can hope for is some sort of acceptance." She paused. "You know, when I didn't get into medical school I think they almost panicked, thinking they might have me at home for another few years. I really think they're ashamed of me."

"Phew!" said Jo through gritted teeth, her hands clenching into tight fists. "How can they be like that? They're monsters, real monsters."

"No, not really," said Lynn. "It's just that everything's so easy for them. They're a sort of golden couple. I never really fitted in. I wasn't clever enough, cute enough, even pretty enough for them. I decided quite early that the best plan for me was to be seen and not heard, to blend into the background as much as I could. I never drew attention to myself, never made trouble or answered back. I wasn't sharp enough to argue with them, anyway." She dabbed her eyes again. "I suppose that's why I'm always tidying up. It's a way of not drawing attention to myself at home. If the house is neat and tidy, if my room's not full of junk, they hardly notice I'm there."

"But that's awful," said Jo. "It's cruel. And why should you want to be like them? It's just arrogant of them to expect you to be a carbon copy of them."

Lynn shrugged. "But they do. Success is everything to them. And if I'm not successful at *something* – well . . ."

Jo thought of her parents again. How different they were – supportive even if Jo or her brother, Tim, failed at something, and always loving, caring – always that. "The rats!" she almost spat. "The unfeeling, short-sighted, cru . . ."

Lynn interrupted her. "I don't think it's done on purpose," she said. "I think they're just really disappointed with me – sometimes I think I can almost see it in their eyes. Sometimes I wonder why they had me at all. I expect they thought they'd produce another Einstein or something – and look what they got – Frankenstein."

Jo laughed. "Hey, that's quite witty. You should try smart talking more often. And remember, you're a free agent now – well, as free as student nurses ever are – so forget them. Don't worry about what they expect of you. You can be a new Lynn here. You can loosen up, stop worrying about being tidy and invisible. Speak up for yourself. Start to enjoy life."

"But I never seem to fit in. I always feel nervous, stupid. I don't feel able to speak out, to fully express myself – whoever *that* may be."

Jo smiled. "Oh, I don't know about that. I seem to remember you spoke up for yourself on our first night. Remember? You told me to get off your case, yes? Called me a slob?"

"How could I forget? I felt awful afterwards, but I didn't know how to make things better again."

"No problem. I think I deserved it, anyway. And I am a slob. But I'm not going to go around apologizing for the way I am – and neither should you."

Lynn threw her paper tissue onto the floor, deliberately missing the wastepaper basket. "There," she said with a small laugh. "My tidy days are over. From now on I'm going to – what's the saying – hang free?"

"Hang loose," said Jo. "Good for you. Forget your parents, and think about enjoying yourself here. That's what I intend to do. And the enjoyment starts tomorrow. It's the Freshers' Ball, remember? That should be good. Come with Nishma and me."

"Oh, no, I couldn't," said Lynn, seemingly gripped by a minor panic.

But Jo wasn't going to give up so easily. "Why not?" she asked.

Lynn hesitated. "Well, the thing is, I've got to wash my . . ."

Jo held up her hand. "Enough," she said. "The only thing you have to wash is you. Chores are over for the weekend." She slammed a textbook shut on the desk. "So is studying. We'll chat and have a drink, and dance — and there are bound to be lots of boys there."

"But I don't know anything about boys. I've hardly spoken to a boy since junior school. And I can't dance, I know I can't."

"Then you can start learning about both," said Jo. "I'm not listening to any arguments, any excuses. You're coming to the Freshers' Ball, and that's final. Okay?"

Lynn nodded. "Okay." She was silent for a few seconds, watching as Jo started to unbutton her uniform. "But, Jo, what will I wear?"

Jo smiled at Lynn. "Now that's more like it!" she said, and flung open the wardrobe doors.

CHAPTER THREE

FRESHERS

The Freshers' Ball was held at the local tennis club. The low roof had been hung with balloons and streamers, and the windows had been covered in black tissue. A DJ's deck had been set up on the stage at one end, and a strobe lighting system threw bands of colour across the people on the dance floor. Madonna was playing at full volume so that Jo had to shout to make herself heard. "Not bad," she shouted into Nishma's ear. "Not bad at all."

Nishma pointed into the far corner. "Look, there's Jenny and Carol and that crowd. Let's join them."

The three girls threaded their way across the dance floor. Jo noticed a few familiar faces, but most of the people were new to her. The disco was open to everyone, so as well as second and third years there were probably lots of people who had nothing to do with St Stephen's.

Jo had hardly sat down at the table when a Deacon Blue track started. "Come on," she said, pulling Nishma to her feet. "Let's dance."

Jo turned as she walked onto the floor. "Coming, Lynn?" she asked.

"What?" Lynn had been gazing into the sea of faces lit up by the strobe lights. "Oh, er, no, not just now," she said.

Jo and Nishma danced together until a slow U2 track came on. "I don't fancy smooching with you," said Jo. "Let's get a drink."

They sat over tall glasses of orange and soda until a Janet Jackson track that Jo liked started up. "Can't miss this one," said Jo. She touched Lynn's arm. "Come on, let's dance."

"No, honestly, I can't, I mean, I don't know how," she said.

Jo looked around the floor. "Look, no one taught them how to dance," she said. "It's not hard. It comes naturally, honestly. And don't imagine everyone will be looking at you, ready to criticize. They won't."

"No, it's just that . . ." Lynn paused, and shook her head. "I'd rather just sit here and watch."

Jo was exasperated. "You can't sit on the sidelines watching all your life, you know," she said. Then she turned away abruptly. "But please yourself."

Jo turned to Nishma. "Come on, the record'll

be over if we don't get out there soon."

When the track was over Nishma looked at Jo. "Can we talk?" she said. "In the ladies?"

The two girls stood in front of the long mirror. "Don't be too hard on Lynn," said Nishma. "I think she feels out of place here. Think what it must be like for her."

"Oh, I know," said Jo. "It's just that she seems so – feeble, at times. I mean, what harm would a dance or two do?"

"No harm at all," said Nishma. "But I wouldn't have said that a year or two ago, you know. My parents aren't as bad as Lynn's – nothing like, really, but they do have great expectations for their children. Most Asian parents do. And they used to be really strict with me. It wasn't until I went to sixth form college that I could even speak to boys, never mind dance with them."

"But look at you now," said Jo.

"Yeah, but it took time for me to feel at ease at discos and places," said Nishma. "I can remember how it felt at first, so I think I know how Lynn's feeling. Just go easy on her, hey? Don't rush it."

Jo looked hard at her reflection. "Okay, I'll cool it. But Lynn's not going to spoil *my* fun. She can sit on the sidelines –" she glanced at the pile of old tennis raquets in the corner, "but I want to be on centre court!"

Back at the table, Jo was chatting to Carol

when she sensed someone standing beside her. She looked up into a pair of blue eyes that looked directly into hers. He was tall, slim, and had sandy hair and freckles. Not my type at all, thought Jo, smiling weakly, knowing what was coming next.

"Would you like to dance?" said the boy, smiling widely.

Jo's face didn't exactly register delight, but she nodded. "Alright."

Jo and the boy danced, then stood at the bar. "You're one of the new first years, aren't you?" said the boy.

Jo glanced down at her dress. "Does it show?"

The boy laughed. "No, not really, but I've seen you around."

"So you're at St Stephen's?"

"Yes, I'm in my third year. Andy Callaghan. Are you doing registered general nursing, too?"

Jo sipped her drink. "That's the plan. But I've only done a week. There's a long way to go yet."

"That's right. But it gets better – and easier, in a way – believe me. Wait till you get on the wards, you'll feel like a real nurse then."

"Yes, I suppose so." Jo put her drink down, and looked up. She'd just had an idea. "Andy? Would you do me a favour? A big favour?"

Andy looked doubtful. "Depends. What is it?"

Jo motioned over to her table in the corner.

"See that girl at the table over there? In the blue skirt and white shirt? Would you ask her to dance?"

"Why?" asked Andy.

"Oh, she's so timid and quiet, she'll sit on that chair all night unless someone gets her off it. Go on, will you? And don't take no for an answer."

"But maybe she's sitting down because she doesn't want to dance. Surely she could dance with your friends if she wanted to?"

Jo sighed. "Yes, she could. But I want *you* to dance with her. As a favour. Will you? Please?"

Now it was Andy's turn to sigh. "No," he said quietly. "I don't like the idea. And what if she finds out that you asked me to dance with her?"

"So what?" said Jo, slamming down her drink this time. "Thanks for the drink — see you around." And she stalked off across the floor.

Jo threw herself down into her chair and glared out at the dancers. Her face was flushed and her jaw set and stern. Lynn touched her shoulder. "What's wrong?" she asked. "You look upset."

"Not upset. Just angry," Jo snapped, not bothering to look at Lynn.

"But what happened?" said Lynn.

"Nothing."

Jo turned around quickly as her shoulder was touched again. "Look, I've just told you. Nothing happened. I don't want to talk . . ."

Jo stopped in mid sentence, her glare turning into a smile. "Sorry, I thought you . . ."

"Want to dance?"

Jo nodded, and followed a tall, dark, good-looking boy onto the floor. As they danced she looked at him more closely. This must be my lucky night, she thought. He's the best-looking guy here. And I bet he's not from St Stephen's. He's far too smart, too well-dressed, and too self-assured. He must be an executive some-thing-or-other.

The record ended and as they stood close together under the lights, Jo asked, "Are you from St Stephen's? A nurse?"

The boy laughed. "Me? A nurse? No way. I'm in marketing. My name's Mark Laurence."

"Jo Carr," said Jo. "I'm a nurse, well a student, at St Stephen's. I've been here a week."

"Which is why you're at the Freshers' Ball, huh?"

Another track started before Jo could reply, and they danced again. In fact, they danced together for the rest of the evening, and when the DJ announced the last record – a smoochy George Michael ballad – Mark held Jo close and they moved slowly around the floor under the flickering lights. Jo closed her eyes and let herself melt against Mark. What was happening? Jo's head was whirling, and it wasn't because of the glass of white wine Mark had bought her. Jo let herself move with the music – with Mark – and hoped the track would never end, it all felt so good.

When the track ended and the floor started to clear, Mark said, "Get your bag. I'll take you home."

Jo sat in Mark's car and felt unsure of herself. She wanted to talk to him, but didn't know what to say; wanted to do something but didn't know what to do. She didn't want to leave him, didn't want the night to end.

Outside the nurses' home Jo put her hand on the car door. "Well, thanks for the lift, Mark. Thanks for a . . ."

She didn't say anything else, for as she looked up Mark's lips closed on hers and his arms were tight around her. The kiss seemed to last forever – but Jo didn't want it to end. When their lips parted Mark still held her close, his shallow breath warm on her neck. Jo didn't open her eyes, afraid that if she did the spell would be broken.

Mark kissed her again, then released her. "Can I see you again, Jo?" he asked.

Can you see me again? Jo thought to herself. Can birds sing? "Yes, I'd like that," she said out loud.

"I'll ring you sometime, okay?"

"Yes," said Jo. "But I'm living in the nurses' home. There's a phone on the corridor, not far from my room. Make sure you ask for me, okay. Jo Carr, remember. I'll be in every night this week."

"Sure." Mark turned the key in the ignition and switched on the lights. "See you, Jo."

The car roared off, leaving Jo standing on the pavement. She watched until the car turned a corner, then turned and ran into the nurses' home. She flung open the door of the communal kitchen and found the others sitting around the table drinking coffee.

"Well, did you see him?" she asked. "Did you see him? Isn't he amazing-looking? And he chose me!" She danced around the table, hugging herself, a beaming smile spreading across her face. "And he wants to see me again. He's going to ring me. His name's Mark Laurence. If any of you answer the phone, make sure you find me, even if I'm in the shower, anywhere, you hear. Oh, he's wonderful, amazing. Can you believe it? *Me* — and Mark Laurence. Brilliant!"

CHAPTER FOUR

WAITING

For the next few days Jo jumped whenever the phone rang outside her room. She took calls from mums, calls from dads, calls from sisters and a call from an irate bank manager. She even took two wrong numbers – but there was no call from Mark.

She grilled everyone, sure that someone had answered Mark's call and forgotten to tell her – or hung up on him. She even stuck up a label on the wall: WANTED – call from Mark Laurence. Contact Jo Carr, room 4. Small reward offered. But it made no difference. By Thursday night, Jo hadn't heard from Mark.

Jo had found it hard to concentrate on her work in the lecture rooms; instead of bones and muscles, her head had been full of Mark. She'd felt so positive that he'd really liked her, really would want to see her again. But now? Now she couldn't think of anything but him. Even the nursing school skeleton – Cedric – seemed to have Mark's face.

It was early evening and Jo was sitting in front of a mug of cold tea and a plate of congealed baked beans. She pushed the beans slowly around the plate with her fork.

Andy came in and sat down opposite her. "Hi," he said. No response. Andy waved a hand in front of Jo's eyes. "Anybody in?"

Jo managed a small smile. "No," she said, hardly glancing up.

"What's wrong?" asked Andy. "Finding the course hard going?"

"No, well, yes, I suppose I am really. You see, I just can't concentrate. Miss McNeil gave me a real blast the other day. I deserved it, I suppose. I couldn't answer her question because I just hadn't been listening."

"But why? D'you think the work's boring?"

"No, it's not that, it's ..." Jo's voice trailed to a whisper, and she looked up into Andy's face. He had kind eyes, a warm smile, and the sort of face you trusted right away. He reminded Jo of her brother, Tim, not in looks, but he had the same open, understanding expression. I can trust him, Jo decided in a split second. And I need someone to talk to. She took a deep breath. "Look, I'm sorry about Saturday night at the Fresher's Ball. It was a stupid idea. Okay? Can we be friends?"

"Sure," said Andy. "Come on. What is it?"

"There's this boy. I met him at the Freshers' Ball, and . . ."

"The one you danced with nearly all night? The one who took you home?"

Jo nodded. "He said he'd ring me, that we'd see each other again. But today's Friday, and he hasn't rung yet. And I'm beginning to think he isn't going to ring."

"So?" said Andy. "It's not as if you had a great relationship going, is it? You only saw him that one night."

"But I really like him," said Jo. "*Really* like him. He's got to ring, he's just got to."

Andy stood up. "Look, there are plenty of other blokes around – like me, for instance. How about . . ."

Andy paused as the phone rang in the hall, and Jo jumped out of her chair. She hurled herself down the hall and grabbed the receiver. "Hello, yes, yes, it's me, Mark." Andy watched as a big cheesy grin split Jo's face from ear to ear. "When? Tonight? Of course – I'd love to. Yes, yes, okay."

Andy stood up and squeezed past Jo. "See you," he said quietly, and pushed open the door. Jo didn't answer – she didn't even notice that he'd gone.

Jo burst into room 4 a few seconds later. "Action stations! Clear the decks!" she called, throwing open the wardrobe doors. She glanced at her face in the long mirror and ran a hand through her hair. "Now, what shall I wear?"

"You sound cheerful," said Lynn, looking up from the books spread out across the desk.

Since the Freshers' Ball the atmosphere had been a bit strained between them, but nothing could dampen Jo's happiness. Not even wet-blanket Lynn, she thought.

Jo hugged herself and a pink flush crept up her neck. "Mark just rang. He's taking me out. Oh, that voice! It does things to me. He has to be the best-looking guy I've ever seen. And he's taking me out tonight. *Me!*" She grabbed her towel from the back of a chair and groped under the bed until she found her washbag. She glanced at Lynn's Mickey Mouse clock. "Oh no, I've only got half an hour!" she said, and disappeared through the door.

Lynn turned back to her books.

CHAPTER FIVE

MARK LAURENCE

Mark took Jo to a new wine bar that had opened in town, *Cheers*. He poured glasses of white wine for each of them and glanced at the menu. "Do you want to eat?" he asked.

"No, I ate earlier," said Jo, thinking back to the untouched baked beans. "We share a kitchen. We can make snacks, but there's the canteen, too. It's . . ."

Mark pulled a face. "Yeuk, canteen food, all fish fingers and mashed potatoes and chips."

Jo felt a little defensive. "It's not like that. There's a good salad bar, and . . ."

A stranger slipped into their booth. "Hi, Mark," he said. He looked at Jo and smiled. "Who's this?"

"Hi, Mike," said Mark. "This is Jo. She's new around here – from St Stephen's."

"Oh, one of the new student nurses, eh?" said Mike smoothly. "You met at the Freshers' Ball, yes? I imagine you enjoyed yourselves."

Mark nodded, but didn't say anything.

Mike smiled at Jo again. "Very nice," he said, and Jo gritted her teeth. How dare he look at her like that? Sizing her up like a pork chop in a butcher's shop window? And that arrogant expression! Jo bit her tongue and took a sip from her wine glass, her eyes flashing angrily over the rim.

Mike stood up. "Well, have a good time," he said to Mark. "You know what they say about nurses." He laughed a laugh that sounded more like a snigger to Jo, and walked off.

Jo turned to Mark. "What *do* they say about nurses?" she asked, trying to keep the anger out of her voice.

Mark saw that she was angry, just the same. "I don't know what 'they' say," he said quietly, looking into her eyes. "But I say they're pretty, and bright – and fun, okay? Well, you are, anyway." He kissed Jo lightly and she felt her anger melt away. How could he have this effect on her? Her legs felt like jelly, and she knew just enough about pulses to realize that hers was racing. She tore her eyes from his and picked up her glass. Was it her imagination, or was her hand shaking? Jo took a large gulp of wine. Calm down, she told herself firmly. Calm down.

When she thought she could trust her voice not to come out like a squeak, she turned back to Mark. "Tell me about your job. Marketing sounds very glamorous."

Mark shrugged. "Not really. But the pay's good. I make a lot of money, and I have a company car, of course. That's useful."

Useful? thought Jo. You bet. Tim had given her a few lessons in his car, but it would be years before she could afford to buy a car of her own, after she was qualified, at least. Suddenly that day seemed an awful long way off.

"You've done well to get so far this early. I mean, you're not very old, are you?"

"Twenty-one," said Mark. "But it's a young man's game. The trick is to move around a lot. If you get slightly more money each time, you soon get into the top league."

Jo's heart lurched. He moved around a lot? Oh, no, please don't let him move away, not now, she panicked. Not when I've just moved here – and am going to be stuck here for the next three years.

"So what do you actually do?" Jo asked. "I mean, I've heard of marketing, but what is it? What do you market?"

"I've just moved to Plastex; they have that big office complex on the bypass. We make drinks receptacles."

Jo didn't know the name. "Drinks receptacles?"

Mark paused for a second. "Plastic cups, actually. You know, for drinks machines, canteens. Plastex are one of the biggest suppliers in the . . ."

Jo laughed. "But how do you market a plastic cup? I would have thought one was much the same as another."

"Yes – but it's our job to persuade people that ours are better, are the ones they should buy. Look, take our new Giganticups. They're thirty per cent bigger than normal, so if people use them in their machines, they sell more drinks, make more profit."

"But what if people don't want thirty per cent more coffee?"

"They leave what they don't want. But profit's the important thing, and if we can promise people higher profits they'll use our cups."

"Oh, I see," said Jo. "I think nursing's more in my line."

"I don't know how you can, really I don't. I mean, I know we all need nurses, but all those old, decrepit people, accident victims and things . . . Ugh!"

Faced with that, Jo would normally have launched into a defence of nursing, but not tonight. She wasn't going to let anything spoil her time with Mark. So, he didn't like the idea of nursing; plenty of people felt like that. And so what? What did her dad say? Horses for courses? Yes. She smiled brightly. "You market, and I'll nurse, okay?"

"Sure," said Mark. "Want some more wine?"

The rest of the evening went quickly, too quickly for Jo's liking. They chatted about everything under the sun. Jo learned a little about Mark's family, and met a couple more of his friends who, she was glad to find, were nothing like oily Mike. Jo told him a little about her family, too, but didn't dwell on that subject; she was missing them anyway, and talking about them made it worse, somehow. She found herself talking about them in the past tense, and they all seemed a long, long way away.

At the end of the evening Mark drove Jo home and stopped the car outside the grounds of the nurses' home. He nodded towards the lighted windows. "Is there a curfew?"

"No, its not exactly Stalag 9, you know. We're supposed to be in by twelve, that's all."

"That gives us plenty of time then," said Mark, and he drew Jo into his arms. They kissed, and Jo felt all the things she'd felt the first time – her heart fluttering, her pulse quickening. And above all, it felt so easy with Mark, so right. She felt safe and secure and warm in his arms, as if it were the only place she ever wanted to be. It was such an intense, strong feeling, she was sure that Mark must feel it too. Their lips parted, and their eyes met — and held for what seemed an eternity. Yes, I'm sure he feels it, thought Jo.

Mark nuzzled his face into Jo's neck. "If only there was somewhere we could go," he said in a low, husky voice.

Jo stiffened slightly. "What do you mean? What for?" Alarm bells had started to ring in her ears.

Mark kissed her earlobe gently. His breath was hot against her skin. "You know, somewhere where we could be alone, get to know each other better."

Jo's voice sounded a little unsure — almost frightened. "But we are alone, and I think the car's just fine for now."

"Mmm," muttered Mark, and pulled Jo towards him again, kissing her hard and long until her head started to spin and she could feel her doubts and feelings of alarm melting away.

"It's a pity you haven't got a flat," he said as they held each other tightly.

Jo felt an irrational urge to apologize, almost. "We have to live in for our first year," she said. "Next year I'll be able to live in a flat, if I can afford it. But . . . but don't you have a flat?" Mark hadn't talked about where he lived, but she had assumed he'd have his own place.

"No, I live at home with the folks. I'm not the domesticated type. Any flat I moved into would have to come complete with housekeeper. I like my creature comforts."

Jo looked at the digital clock on the dashboard and thought for the first time in hours about tomorrow. It was a full day — and after her performance earlier in the week, Miss McNeil would be gunning for her. And she hadn't done the work they had all been set. "Look, I'd better go in now, Mark. It's late, I've got work to do, and I have to be up early."

Mark gently nuzzled Jo's neck and she shivered very slightly. "I do wish you wouldn't do that," she said.

Mark laughed. "Why, don't you like it?"

"You know I like it!" said Jo, pulling away. "But I must go in."

Mark held up his hands. "Okay, you win." He leaned across Jo and released the door. Jo wanted to ask when they'd see each other again, but couldn't force the words out. "Will we, will I . . ." she stuttered.

Mark kissed her gently and glanced in the mirror before switching on his lights and turning the key in the ignition. "I'll ring you," he said, and then Jo clambered out of the car. She stood on the pavement, watching, as the car roared off along the road.

"Please ring me," she said, turning away only when the car's lights had disappeared. "Please."

CHAPTER SIX

DE MILO'S

The next few weeks passed almost in a blur for Jo – but a happy, blissful, loving blur. She spent almost all her off-duty time with Mark, and they were soon regarded as a couple. Most of the friends they saw accepted them as Mark-and-Jo, and it was always assumed that they'd be seen together. Wine bars, restaurants, the squash club and the cinema – they went everywhere together. Even after weeks, Jo could hardly believe her luck in meeting Mark. They'd never mentioned the word love – but Jo had no doubt that she was in love with Mark, and hoped that, even if he didn't feel that serious about her now, it would come in time.

Jo had little or no time for anything or anyone else. She chatted to Lynn, of course, and to Nishma and the others on the corridor – but it was usually as she was coming in or going out, or as they sat over lunch in the canteen.

She saw quite a lot of Andy; he was always around. He seemed to get on with everyone in the hospital, and Jo could see why – he was easy-going, witty, and was always cheerful. He was also always ready to lend an ear to anyone with a problem, and Jo found him filling the gap in her life that her leaving home had caused. There, big brother Tim, had always been ready with no-nonsense advice and a shoulder to cry on; with no Tim to turn to, Jo confided in Andy.

Not that she felt she had many problems – not with Mark, at least. Jo's problems were more practical ones. Her work on the course wasn't going well, and people – people who mattered, like Miss McNeil – were starting to notice. She'd already had a few low-key warnings about making more effort, trying harder, putting in more homework, but they hadn't made much impact.

Jo knew that her work was important, that she could fail the course and have to leave – but how could she refuse to go out with Mark when he asked her? There just didn't seem enough hours in the day to fit everything in – and Jo chose to make time for Mark rather than her work. Jo was always with Mark – and that's how she liked it.

When Nishma knocked and walked into Room 4 one Saturday afternoon she was sur-prised to see Jo there, lying on her bed reading a magazine. "What are you doing here? We usually hardly see you between Friday night and Monday morning. Ah, what it must be like to have such a hectic social life."

"Ha, ha," said Jo in a stage laugh. "Mark's at a sales do this weekend, so I won't be seeing him. It's in Birmingham, and he won't be back until Monday."

"Shame. Still, I think we can fill a few empty hours for you."

"Oh, yeah?"

"Yeah. I've persuaded most of the girls to come out for a pizza tonight, at that new place near the precinct – De Milo's. Come with us."

"I don't know," said Jo. "I've got a lot of work to do. McNeil had another dig at me yesterday. I've got to knuckle down to some work or she'll be gunning for me again next week."

Nishma sat on the bed beside Jo and flicked the magazine closed. "Oh, yeah, you're working very hard, aren't you? I hate to break the news, Jo, but this is not an anatomy textbook."

Jo sighed. "I know. I just can't seem to get down to work today."

Nishma jumped up and pulled Jo to her feet. "Do it tomorrow, then," she said, "fortified by pizza and red wine. Will you come? Go on, we haven't had a night out for ages."

Just then Lynn came in, her head wrapped in a

towel. "Are you going on this night out?" Jo asked her.

"You know, a pizza at De Milo's," Nishma added. "Remember, we talked about it yesterday. Carol and the others are all going."

Lynn started to rub her hair with the towel. "I don't know. I've got a lot to do." She jerked her thumb towards the desk, which was piled high with books.

"Work, work, work," said Nishma. "Come on, Lynn, you won't be thrown off the course just for not studying every hour God sends, you know. Look at Jo — she's way behind on her course work, but she's coming."

"I am?" said Jo.

"You are."

Jo picked up her magazine and flicked through the pages. "Let's see if it's in the stars, shall we?"

Nishma groaned. "If you must."

Jo read aloud from the magazine. "Colour red, initials P and S, that doesn't mean anything to me. If an unexpected invitation comes your way — accept it."

"You're joking," said Nishma. "Does it really say that?"

Jo held out the magazine. "Yes — look, here. But it might mean Mark — maybe he's going to ring and take me out."

Nishma shook her head. "Very unlikely. He's

in Birmingham until Monday, isn't he? No, it must mean us." She picked up a scarf and held it across her face. "We are your destiny — Gipsy Rose Nishma predicts it. Ignore my words at your peril."

Jo pulled the scarf from Nishma's face. "Idiot," she said, and turned to Lynn. "I'll go if you do."

"Okay."

Nishma was already at the door. "Great," she said over her shoulder. "See you at the front door at eight."

De Milo's was cheap and cheerful, all red-checked tablecloths, dark green paintwork and candles in bottles. But the food was good, and Jo was almost surprised to realize just how much she was enjoying herself. She'd imagined she'd feel at a loss without Mark, they'd spent so much time together, but she was having a good time — though it did feel just a little strange to have Lynn sitting beside her in a restaurant, not Mark.

"What did you think of the practical on Tuesday?" asked Lynn.

A loud series of groans was the only reply she got.

Nishma held up her finger. "Rule one of tonight's meeting," she said sternly. "No talk of catheters or spleens, or . . ."

"Bed pans?" said Carol.

Nishma nodded. "Quite. You can talk about anything, Lynn, anything under the sun, *except* work and nursing, okay?"

Lynn smiled. "It's just that I don't have much else to talk about."

"Then we'll have to do something about that," Nishma replied. "Tear you away from that desk more often. Show you life *outside* St Stephen's. Eh, Jo?"

"That's right," said Jo. "This is a pretty good town, you know. There's lots going on. Mind you, I'd enjoy living in Timbuctoo as long as Mark was around."

Lynn looked down at her napkin. "Mmm, but I haven't got a Mark, remember?"

"Well, you'll have to find one," said Carol. "After I've found my ideal man, of course."

"But I don't seem to have the time to go out," said Lynn. "There are always things to do."

"You have to find time," said Nishma. She looked at Jo. "I mean, Jo has as much work as the rest of us, but it doesn't cramp her style, does it? She's out nearly every night of the week these days."

Jo groaned loudly. "Don't remind me, *please*. You know what trouble I'm in with the McNeil. She's really after me. Look, shut up, I don't want to think about it, all right?"

"Don't want to think about what?" said a voice

as Andy appeared at Jo's shoulder.

"Oh, hi, Andy, I didn't know you were here."

Andy waved to a corner booth. "We've just come in." He bent closer to Jo's face. "Don't want to think about what?"

Jo sighed and pulled a 'must I?' face, but Andy didn't take the hint. "What's wrong?" he asked.

"It's clan chief McNeil. She had me in her office the other day to give me a stern talking to. Reminded me how far behind with my work I was — as if I needed reminding — and said I'd have to improve, or . . ." Jo spread her hands in front of her and shrugged her shoulders.

"Or what?" said Andy.

"She said . . ."

"I don't want to hear what she said," said Nishma, interrupting. "We just agreed that St Stephen's, nursing, and Miss McNeil in particular are not up for discussion tonight, Andy. Now that's the rules, okay?"

The waiter came to take their order and Jo realized that she hadn't even glanced at the menu. "We did agree," she said. "So . . ."

"So I'll see you later, over in the Feathers, yes?"

"Great," said Jo, and as Andy made his way to his table, she turned her attention to the menu.

The Feathers was one of the quieter pubs in town

– it had a juke box in one room, but there were quieter areas where it was possible to talk over the sound of the music. Andy and his friends had found a small table and collected a group of low stools around it. They were about the only seats left in the place.

Andy waved as the girls looked around. "Over here!" he called. "Come on, hurry up, you lot. We've had to guard these seats with our lives."

The girls weaved through the other groups in the room and sat around the table. "I'll get the drinks," said Nishma, and headed off for the bar. "Come on, Lynn," she said over her shoulder. "You can help me carry them."

"Phew!" said Carol. "What a blow out. Why couldn't I resist the zabaglione? The pizza was filling, but I had to down another five hundred calories."

"I think they hit you with the dessert list when you're weakest," said Jo. "They fill you with garlic bread and pizza until you're satisfied and full and complacent and relaxed, then they tempt you with ice-cream sundaes and cheesecakes and things." She adopted her Miss Jean Brodie accent. "One is powerless to resist." She waved her arms around the table. "At least, my girls are."

Ian's face wore a mock self-righteous look.

"We left after our pizzas, I hope you noticed," he said. "Strong in the face of temptation, that's us."

"Huh, I bet if they'd had bread and butter pudding on the menu you'd still be over there, having second helpings. I saw you in the canteen queue the other day. Drooling, you were, positively drooling."

Ian smiled at the memory. "Ah, well, that's different."

When Nishma and Lynn got back from the bar, Andy stood up. "Here, take my seat, Nishma," he said. "I want to talk to Jo."

Nishma rolled her eyes. "And I thought you were being gallant."

Andy sat down on the stool next to Jo's. "Well," he said. "What did she say?"

"Nishma? She said she thought you were being . . ."

"No, not Nishma. You know what I'm talking about. Miss McNeil, you know, your nurse tutor? What did she have to say to you?"

Jo adopted her genteel Scots accent; she was getting good at it. "Well, she wasnae verrry happy wi' me," she said.

But Andy wasn't laughing this time. "Don't joke about it all the time, Jo," he said. "It sounded pretty serious. Was it? Are you really in trouble?"

"Okay, no jokes. And I think it is pretty serious — or it very soon could be. She isn't very happy with me, she really isn't."

"But what happened? What did she say?"

"Are you sitting comfortably? Then I'll begin," said Jo, but after another look at Andy's serious, concerned face, she began again. "Sorry. I just have to make a joke of it, or . . ." She shrugged her shoulders. "It just seems easier not to think about it."

"Think about what?"

"Okay, I'll start at the beginning, cross the t's and dot the i's," said Jo, and drew a deep breath. "Well, you know we've been doing a lot more practical work these last few weeks? Been on the wards more?"

Andy nodded. "Yeah, go on."

"Well, I've been enjoying it, I really have. I really like the contact with the patients. I mean, it's nerve-racking when you start out, it feels awkward handling someone else; I was frightened of hurting someone. But it got better — and I suppose it's the same for all of us. But Miss McNeil told me she didn't think my work was good enough. She doesn't think I'm putting in enough effort. She says I'm not concentrating, that my mind is elsewhere."

"But what have you actually done wrong?"

"Nothing really drastic. It's just a few silly mistakes — putting a 'nil by mouth' card over the wrong patient, losing my way when she told me to take something to the path lab. Things like that. I mean no one was in any danger or anything, you know how close the supervision is — I think she just doesn't sort of trust me. Thinks I'm muddle-headed, scatty. And I suppose I am."

Andy shook his head. "Those are the sort of mistakes everyone makes at the start of training. They're small things. Surely Miss McNeil wouldn't come down on you just for that?"

"Ah, well, there is something else," said Jo. "It's my written work, my assignments. I'm way behind with them, and she's been nagging me to keep up almost since the start. I seemed to fall behind right away, and it's getting worse."

"Do you find the theory hard?" said Andy. "It takes time to become . . ."

"No, not hard exactly. When I sit down and work it all seems pretty straightforward. It's just finding the time. And I do prefer the practical work. It seems more like what nursing should be about, a 'hands on' experience rather than years spent pouring over textbooks. When we've had a full day in the nursing school the last thing I want to do at night is to work through more lectures."

"But it's important, Jo, you know that. The textbook stuff is what will make you a better nurse eventually. Okay, you can deal out tender loving care without much training, but nursing's about a great deal more than that."

Jo looked as though she'd heard all that before, and she had – from Miss McNeil.

"I know. Miss McNeil said she just didn't think I was putting in enough effort, working hard enough, trying. 'Nursing's not an easy option, you know, Josephine,' she said. 'It's hard, demanding work.' She also said the training's the hardest part. And I think she's right."

"So why aren't you putting in the work, Jo?" Andy asked. "The others seem to be managing."

"Yes, but they aren't going out with Mark."

"Oh, him. But why should he affect your work?"

"Well, we go out a lot; you know that already. I just don't seem to have time to work in the evenings and at weekends. But if I don't I'll never get through the course."

"You won't," said Andy. "You definitely won't. But look, Jo, you don't have to work every off-duty hour to keep up. Nurses don't have to give up having a social life. You just have to balance work and play. Everyone does, not just nurses."

"Yes. Yes, I know the theory," said Jo. "I just find it hard to put into practice. I can't keep saying no when Mark asks to see me, or I'll end up losing him."

Andy looked incredulous. "But what sort of a relationship do you have with him? Surely he knows you're training, that you've got to study in the evenings? I can't believe he'd drop you just because you aren't able to see him every night."

"I suppose not," said Jo, but her face looked doubtful. "It's just that I won't take that chance. I really like Mark, *really* like him, and I can't bear the thought of losing him. He's the most important thing in my life."

Andy stared into his empty glass. "Oh." Then he looked up. "You didn't tell Miss McNeil about him, did you? You didn't make him your excuse for falling behind with the course work?"

"I did mention him. I mean, he is the real reason my work's suffering, I suppose."

"And?"

"She wasn't exactly impressed. Said I couldn't let him take precedence over my work. Said I should attend to my training first and boyfriends second. Said it didn't show much commitment on my side if I concentrated more on my social life than I did on my training, said I'd have to get my priorities right. Think seriously about whether I'm cut out for nursing."

"Phew. Heavy stuff."

"Yes. It made me think, I can tell you."

"And have you come to a decision? Have you decided what to do?"

"I still want to nurse; I've wanted to for as long as I can remember. I'll just have to work harder, try more, convince Miss McNeil that I've got what it takes. If I have."

"You have," said Andy. "You'll just have to knuckle down. Look, I'll help if you like, shall I? Help you to catch up?"

Jo shook her head. "No, I think it's something I've got to do myself." She drained her glass. "And I'm going to start first thing tomorrow. Mark's away for the weekend, so I'm going to use the time to get some serious work done."

"But what about when he gets back? Will it be back to normal, out till all hours every night, no time for studying?"

Jo laughed. "You're beginning to sound like Miss McNeil! No, I'll just have to divide my time better — less for Mark, more for study."

Now it was time for Andy to adopt a Miss Jean Brodie accent. "That's ma girrl," he said.

Jo laughed. "Idiot!"

She glanced at her watch. "Well, if I'm to spend all day working I'd better get a good night's sleep." She stood up. "Anyone walking back?"

The others decided to have another drink, except Nishma, and the two girls set off for the nurses' home together.

"What were you and Andy talking about so

intently?" asked Nishma as they walked. "Or shouldn't I ask?"

"Ask away," said Jo. "We were just talking about the dressing-down Miss McNeil gave me last week. I haven't seen Andy since then."

"He cares a lot about you, doesn't he?"

"Does he?" said Jo, then, "Yes, I suppose he does. We're mates. I like him a lot. We get on well. But it's nothing special — he talks to you, too, doesn't he?"

"Usually only to ask where you are," said Nishma. "You must know how he feels about you. It's obvious to everyone else, believe me. Go on, admit it."

"Admit what? There's nothing to admit. We're mates, that's all."

"I think it's more than that — as far as Andy's concerned, anyway."

"What do you mean?"

"I mean that I think Andy would like you to be more than friends."

"What? That's rubbish. And anyway, Andy knows that Mark's my boyfriend, and will be for the foreseeable future, if I have anything to do with it. Like I said, Andy's a mate, that's all."

CHAPTER SEVEN

INTRODUCTIONS

Jo sat down at the table in the crowded canteen. She had just started to eat her salad when Lynn joined her.

"Where's Nishma?" asked Jo. "Not eating in today?"

"I'm not sure." She looked across the sea of faces. "There she is, in the queue at the salad bar." She stood up and waved. "Nishma, Nishma. Over here."

Jo paused, her fork halfway to her mouth. "Who did you get for special study?" she asked.

Lynn smiled. "Oh, a lovely man called Mr Roberts. He had a stroke a few weeks ago. But he doesn't let it get him down. He's got some paralysis on his left side, but he's determined to get better. He's old, almost eighty, but you'd never think it. He's bright and funny. And really easy to talk to. He's having some problems with his speech, with some facial paralysis, but he's working really hard at getting back to normal. Sister thinks he should be able to go home quite soon. He'll manage with some support, a home help, meals on wheels, things like that."

"You're lucky," said Jo. "He sounds really sweet." And easy, she thought. Unlike Nigel Weston . . .

When Miss McNeil had told the student nurses that they were each to be given a special patient to study, Jo had looked forward to the experience. Miss McNeil explained that they had to spend time with 'their' patient, building up a relationship, taking a special interest in their treatment and well-being. At the end of the study period the students would prepare a sort of patient profile, concerned with the medical and surgical care they'd had, the type of nursing they'd needed, but also with their state of mind, their attitudes to the staff and their feelings on the time they'd spent in hospital.

"This sounds like something I can really get my teeth into," she'd told Andy. "When you're doing a hundred little separate jobs all day it's hard to build up a real relationship with the patients – there never seems to be enough time to sit and talk to them properly. This project sounds really very interesting. Worthwhile, somehow."

"I think you'll enjoy it," Andy had said. "I still remember my first case study. An old lady, a spinster who'd broken her hip badly. For lots of people it would have been a good excuse to sit back and grow old gracefully, but not Miss Clayton. She just wanted to be up and about again to look after her goats. She was really spunky, sharp and funny. And you should have heard her swear. She taught me a few new words, I can tell you. I still get a card from her at Christmas. And she's still got her goats."

"I hope I get someone like that," Jo had said.

But she hadn't.

"The patient who will form the basis of your special study is Nigel Weston," Miss McNeil had told Jo. "He's nineteen, and he's been in here for some six weeks. He had a bad motorbike accident. He suffered concussion and spinal injuries as well as cuts and bruises. The superficial injuries have cleared up now, of course, and the concussion, but . . ." She paused and glanced down at the notes in her folder. "Spinal injuries are always difficult to predict. It's likely he'll have a certain degree of disability, but how much of a disability, well . . ."

"But he will walk again?" said Jo. "He's not paralysed?" The thought of a young motorbiker suddenly being confined to life in a wheelchair was a very uncomfortable one. She thought of what it would be like if it happened to her brother, Tim, just a couple of years older. He'd be devastated, destroyed. Jo felt a sudden surge of sorrow and sympathy for Nigel Weston.

"He's not paralysed," said Miss McNeil. "But he's going to have to work hard at getting his mobility back."

"How will he . . ."

"That's for you to find out," said Miss McNeil, interrupting and snapping the file shut before passing it across the table to Jo. "Here are the facts. Now go and meet the real person, the patient. Talk, ask questions – change Nigel Weston from a sheaf of case notes into a real person. Understand?"

Jo nodded. "Yes," she said, picking up the file. Already she was looking forward to meeting Nigel, to put flesh on the bones of the case notes.

The sister on the small spinal injuries unit had pointed to a bed in the corner when Jo had asked if she could see Nigel Weston. "Over there. That's him, in the corner."

"Can I? I mean, will it be all right to?" Jo had said, unsure of herself suddenly.

"Yes, of course, go over. Go on. He won't bite you – well, not very hard, anyway."

Jo took a few steps across the ward. "Good luck," the sister said as she went out through the swing doors.

Jo was still pondering her words when she found herself standing by Nigel Weston's bed. Nigel was dressed in hospital issue pyjamas and an old dressing gown, and he was sprawled on the bed, his back to the rest of the ward, facing the corner. He was turning the pages of a motorbike magazine, Jo could see that, but he seemed unaware of Jo's presence.

Jo panicked a little. How to begin? Should she introduce herself? Cough? Say excuse me? Make a noise so that he would look up? In the end Jo got what she thought was a flash of inspiration.

"That looks like a mean machine," she said.

As soon as the words had left her lips Jo regretted them. What a stupid thing to say! How corny! She sounded like the script of a really low-budget teen film. Mean machine! It sounded like someone trying to communicate with a being from another planet, like an old duchess trying to get on terms with a young skinhead.

She did succeed in breaking the silence, though. Nigel Weston looked up for a second. His face was set, stern, and he barely glanced at Jo. "Sure." It was more grunt than speech.

Jo decided that she would have to try again. She'd got off to a bad start, but there must be a way of making contact. After all, Nigel Weston wasn't an old pensioner, was he? He wasn't someone she had nothing at all in common with.

He was almost the same age, nineteen, and well, she knew a bit about bikes, thanks to Tim. If I can't talk to him, I can't talk to anyone, she told herself sternly. Come on, speak.

"I'm Jo, Jo Carr," she said. "I'm a nurse here, well a student. I've just started this . . ."

Nigel looked up. "I can see you're a nurse." He glanced at the uniform. "What do you want?"

"Nothing, well, nothing officially, that is."

"Go away then."

Jo's eyes opened wider. "What? What did you just say?"

Nigel turned to face Jo. Still there was no trace of a smile. "Watch my lips," he said quietly. "Go," pause, "away."

Jo felt her face redden. Jo had often heard the phrase 'words fail me', but she hadn't known what it really meant — until now. She just didn't know what to say, and stood staring at her shoes, her head spinning.

Nigel looked up from his magazine again. "You still here?"

"Yes, I am," said Jo in what she hoped sounded like a firm, no-nonsense voice. "I'm doing a patient study, it's part of my training. We — that's my group of students — we've all got to write a study on a special patient."

"So?"

"So, you're my special patient," said Jo. "I'm

going to write a case study, you know, about your case, your treatment, that sort of thing."

"No you're not," said Nigel, turning back to his magazine.

"But, but, look, it just means a few hours, you know, chatting, answering questions, that sort of thing."

"No it doesn't," said Nigel, not even bothering to turn around this time. "Because I'm not going to talk. I'm not going to answer any questions. I don't want to be part of your studies. Go and practise on someone else. Go and annoy some other poor bloke."

"But, look – Nigel – I've got to . . ."

Nigel shut the magazine and threw it onto his locker. He put his head on his pillow and looked at the wall a few inches from his face. "Just go away, will you?" he said. This time his voice was softer, low and sad-sounding. "Leave me alone."

Now Jo really was lost for words, and she turned away, walking softly across the floor. She knocked on the door of the sister's office. "Come in," said a voice.

"Oh, it's you," said the sister. "How did you get on?"

Jo would never have admitted it, but she was close to tears. "I didn't," she said.

"I'm not entirely surprised," said the sister. "He's, well, shall we say, prickly?"

"I'd say definitely prickly," said Jo. "Is he very ill? In pain?"

"Most of the pain is in his mind," said the sister. "Nigel can't accept that he might not make a full, one hundred per cent recovery; he might have a limp, for instance. He'll have to work hard, do lots of physiotherapy, for instance, but it's difficult to motivate him. He's very down, very pessimistic at the moment."

"He wouldn't even talk to me," said Jo.

"Come in another time. Try again," said the sister.

"Mmm," said Jo, going to the door. "Thanks."

Jo had gone back to her room, thrown the case notes down on the bed, and thrown herself on the bed, too. This was something I thought I was going to be able to do really well, she said to herself. Something I'd be good at. Something that would convince Miss McNeil that I'm not wasting her time. And what happens? My patient won't even talk to me!

Jo thumped the pillow hard. Damn Nigel Weston, she said to herself. Damn him.

"Hey, wake up, Jo," said Nishma, touching Jo's arm. "You've been staring at that piece of lettuce for the last three minutes. "Is there a caterpillar in it? If so, keep quiet, or everyone else will want one, too."

Jo put the lettuce in her mouth. "Very funny."

"You know what they say — the old jokes are always the best. Well, it's what I say, anyway."

"Mmmm."

"What's wrong? Has Miss McNeil been giving you a hard time again?"

"No, it's not that. She's been okay really, I don't think she bears grudges." A sudden thought flashed across Jo's brain. "Or does she?" What if Miss McNeil had given her Nigel Weston on purpose, knowing that he wouldn't co-operate? What if she'd chosen him specially so Jo would fail to turn in a good paper?

Jo banished the thought from her mind. No, I can't believe she'd do that, she told herself. She wouldn't, she couldn't. No one could be that cruel, no one. I must be getting paranoid.

"What are you on about?" said Nishma.

"Oh, I'm just miserable about the boy they've given me for this special report we've got to write. He won't speak to me, hardly looked up when I went to see him yesterday."

"That's a bit rough. What are you going to do about it?"

"I don't know. Maybe I'll ask Miss McNeil to give me another patient. One who communicates in words of more than one syllable."

"Don't you think it might be better to try again, try to talk to this boy?" Lynn suggested.

"I suppose so," said Jo. "But you don't know what he was like, honestly. I could have strangled him, I really could."

"Not the best way to treat your patients," said Nishma. "But I agree with Lynn. Go and see him again. Maybe he was just in a bad mood."

"A bad mood? If that was a bad mood I wouldn't like to see him in a real temper. And it's all right for you two – you've got the charming old Mr Roberts and co-operative Mrs Lyons." Suddenly Jo's face brightened. "Hey, would either of you like to swap patients? I mean, I wouldn't mind, and . . ."

"No thanks," said Lynn.

"No thanks. Definitely," said Nishma.

"I thought so. I thought so."

Nishma smiled. "Hey, didn't your horoscope say something about an interesting stranger? Who could play a prominent role in your life?"

"Yes, it did," said Jo. "Why?"

"Maybe it's Nigel."

"Oh, funny. Very funny."

CHAPTER EIGHT

A CHANGE OF PLAN

Jo agonized about how to approach Nigel again. Should she adopt a softly-softly approach, or a more confident, aggressive one? What would make him respond? More to the point, would anything she did make him respond? There's only one way to find out, she told herself, and decided to confront him again.

In her first free period she went down to the spinal injuries unit. This time she left her file behind. She hoped it would make her look less official, less nurse-like, even.

She knocked on the sister's office door and met her on the way out. "Can I speak to Nigel?" she said. "I've decided to try again."

The sister shook her head. "Bad timing, I'm afraid. Nigel's down in the pool, having physio." She glanced at her watch. "He'll be another forty minutes, at least. But you're welcome to speak to him then, anytime, in fact."

"Oh," said Jo. "I'll be back in the lecture room by then. But I'll try again another day. Thanks."

Jo looked so dispirited, her shoulders drooping as if in defeat, that she aroused a sense of real sympathy in the sister. "Look," she called, as Jo turned away, "don't feel depressed about your lack of success with Nigel. We all find it very hard to make contact with him at the moment. He's like this with everyone. I think he's very hurt and very frightened about his future, but he won't admit it. He's hiding his fear behind aggression."

"I see," said Jo. "At least, I think I do. I can almost imagine how frightened he is, not knowing if he'll really get better or not."

"Oh, he will get better, I'm sure of that," said the sister. "But we have to work hard together – the team here, and Nigel himself. And if he's optimistic rather than pessimistic, looks forward rather than back, I'm sure he'll get back to normal all the more quickly. Maybe you can help make him see that? You're about his age – maybe you can get through to him."

"I haven't made a very good start," said Jo. "He told me to get lost."

"Look, I've got an idea. Nigel doesn't usually get many visitors at visiting time, you know; his family live quite a way away and they can only get to see him every four or five days. So why don't you come then and visit him?"

"You mean at visiting time?"

"Yes. Why not? Don't come as a nurse doing a patient study, but as a girl who might be willing to be a friend. It might work."

"Yes, I will," said Jo, suddenly brightening. "Thanks, Sister. Thanks a lot."

"That's all right. And let me know how you get on, will you?"

"Of course I will. Thanks again."

Jo had arranged to see Mark that night, at seven thirty – just when visiting time began. She tried to ring him, but couldn't reach him at the office, and when she tried his home his mother told her that she wasn't expecting to see him until much later. "Isn't he seeing you, Jo?" she asked.

"Yes, but I want to get a message to him before that. Never mind, I'll explain when I see him tonight."

Jo rushed to the newsagent's kiosk and bought a new issue of an American biking magazine. A peace offering, she told herself hopefully.

At seven thirty Jo was standing outside the gates, looking for Mark's car. When she saw it she waved, and he pulled into the lay-by.

She kissed him hurriedly. "Look, will you do me a favour, a big favour?"

Jo looked bright, excited, her eyes sparkling.

"That depends," he said, smiling and taking her in his arms. "That depends."

Jo pulled away. "I know you wanted to see that new Jack Nicholson film tonight, but could we do something else?"

"Sure, if you like. What?"

"Visit someone in hospital. Here at St Stephen's."

"But who? Is someone ill? Nishma or someone?"

"No, it's a boy called Nigel. He had a motorbike accident, and he's been in here for weeks. His family live miles away and he doesn't get many visitors, so . . ."

"So you thought you'd do your Florence Nightingale bit and act the angel of mercy, did you?"

"Er, well, yes it is something like that, I suppose," said Jo.

"What's he like? How well do you know this Nigel?"

"Er, I don't know a lot about him, to tell the truth. I don't really know him at all. You see, we've all got these patient case studies to write up — a special in-depth study of one particular patient — and Nigel's my patient. But he's a bit, well, surly, I suppose you could call it. He won't speak to me, won't go along with the study." She laughed a small, strained laugh. "In fact, he told me to shove off last time I spoke to him."

Mark's eyebrows lifted a centimetre. "What? He won't speak to you? And you want to visit him, make small talk with someone you don't know and I've never clapped eyes on?"

"Yes, I just thought that, well, it might be easier if . . ."

"I don't think so, Jo."

Jo sighed. "Please, Mark. It's important. It's a big part of my course work. You know I've been told to work harder – or else. A good case study could make a big difference."

"But you're not on duty now, Jo – and I'm not a nurse. What do they expect of you? Devotion to duty twenty-four hours a day?"

"No, but, well, nursing isn't just another job, is it? It's special, different."

"Sure, it's badly paid, hard work, you're expected to study all the time, take exams. And what about when you start working shifts, night duty? That'll be great, won't it?"

Jo had thought about it. "We'll just have to see each other when we can," she said weakly.

"Great."

Mark looked away and Jo's heart gave a sudden lurch. Don't let me lose him, she said grimly to herself. Don't let anything change. She touched his arm. "Mark?"

He turned and saw that tears were starting to

form in Jo's eyes. He gathered her into his arms and held her close, pressing her hard against him. "I'm sorry," he said. "I just want to be with you always."

"Me too."

"I'm sorry."

"Me too."

Mark laughed. "Don't keep saying that, okay? Now are we going to visit this Nigel bloke?"

An instant picture formed in Jo's mind: Nigel, lying on his bed, his face turned from her, his body tense and somehow arrogant. Then she heard his words, or lack of them, his refusal to speak to her. He had made her feel small, stupid, humiliated. Why should she put herself out for him? Why should she bother? He'd probably behave in just the same way, but this time he'd ignore Mark, too.

She made a decision. "Come on, if we hurry, we can still make the start of the film."

"But what about this bloke, your case study, or whatever it is?"

"There are more important things – you, for instance. I'll worry about the case study tomorrow." She pulled the seatbelt across her chest and snapped it shut. "Come on, you've got about four minutes to get us to the multiscreen."

Mark started the engine. "Right. And, Jo – thanks."

Jo threw back her head and laughed. "Me too!"

When Jo got back to the nurses' home later, Lynn was already in bed, reading. "Hi, how did it go with Nigel?" she asked.

"It didn't."

"You mean he still wouldn't talk to you? Not even with Mark there?"

"No, I mean I didn't go to see Nigel."

"But why? I thought that . . ."

"Then you thought wrong," said Jo, pulling off her shirt and flinging it into a corner. Her tone of voice made Lynn wary of asking any more questions, and she put down her book, lay down, and snapped off her bedside light.

Jo went over to the washbasin, washed her face and dragged a brush through her hair. As she brushed her teeth she looked at herself in the mirror. Her eyes looked troubled, uneasy. What she hadn't said to Lynn, couldn't admit to Lynn, was that she'd spent the entire two hours in the cinema staring at the film on the screen, but instead of seeing the face of Jack Nicholson and the rest of the cast, she'd seen Nigel Weston's face, bleak and sad and hurt. She had tried to blink away the image of his face, to concentrate on the film, but had failed miserably. She had felt unsure and maybe a little ashamed of herself, and thought that she really should have visited

Nigel, as she'd planned. Thinking about him continually had spoiled the evening.

Mark seemed to have picked up her mood, too, and had been quiet and withdrawn. They had had very little to say to each other, and even their kisses in the car when he'd driven her home had felt strained and tense. Jo had felt almost relieved when it was time to part.

Jo got into bed and put out the light. "Goodnight," said Lynn.

"'Night," said Jo, and stared hard into the darkness. Her head was spinning. What was she going to do about Nigel? And what must Mark be thinking of her at this moment? Probably that she'd been sulking and moody because he'd complained about visiting Nigel. But she hadn't been sulking, well, not intentionally, anyway. She'd just slipped into a defeated, demoralized mood, and hadn't been able to drag herself out of it. But why hadn't she told Mark how she was feeling? Maybe asked him to help again? Talked to him? He was her boyfriend, after all, wasn't he, the person closest to her?

Jo realized that she would have felt wary of talking about Nigel again because Mark seemed to resent her work, her career. He seemed to feel that nursing came between them, was spoiling things between them. He'd even talked about working shifts and how that would affect them, and seemed annoyed, hadn't he?

Jo sighed. She felt tired, drained, but knew that sleep would be a long time coming that night – if it came at all . . .

Damn Nigel Weston, she said under her breath. Damn him. And damn St Stephen's, too.

CHAPTER NINE

UNCERTAINTIES

Jo's face was grey and ashen in the morning. She rushed into the lecture room when all the others were already sitting down. "Sorry I'm late, I . . ." she mumbled, and her voice trailed off as Miss McNeil barely glanced up. Her expression said quite clearly that she wasn't in the least surprised to find that it was Jo who was late; it was becoming quite a regular occurrence.

The class started, and Jo had to make a real effort to keep her eyes open. She had spent hours tossing and turning, her mind in turmoil, and now that she had to concentrate, had to stay awake, she felt she could have easily slept the day away.

Through the lecture she found herself staring at the wall behind Miss McNeil's head, looking but not really seeing, listening but not really hearing; certainly not taking anything in. Miss McNeil's words became a blur, a distant hum, until Jo heard two words that pulled her out of her dream-like state.

"Nurse Carr."

Jo blinked, tried to focus properly.

"Nurse Carr!"

Nishma nudged Jo's elbow and looked at her pleadingly. "Jo!" she said out of the side of her mouth.

Jo straightened herself up and looked at her tutor. "Er, yes, Miss, er . . ."

"Have you heard a word I've said in the last fifteen minutes?" said Miss McNeil.

Jo realized she was staring defeat in the face. It was no use lying. One pertinent question from the tutor would reveal the truth. She decided on honesty. "No, Miss McNeil," she said.

"Then I suggest you wake up, and pay attention to the rest of the lecture. You might just learn something. That's what you're here for, after all." She paused. "Isn't it?"

"Yes," Jo mumbled, taking the top off her pen and opening her notebook. She looked up at Miss McNeil. "Sorry."

But Miss McNeil had turned to a chart on the wall behind her. She didn't appear to have heard . . .

At the end of the class the students filed out. "I bet you're glad that's over," Nishma said quietly to Jo.

Jo managed a small, weak smile. "You bet. Trust me to . . ."

"Nurse Carr! Would you go to my office? Right away? I'll join you in a moment." It was Miss McNeil's voice, cold and businesslike.

"It's not over yet," Jo whispered to Nishma, and instead of heading for the canteen with the others, she turned towards the nurse tutor's office.

Miss McNeil was seconds behind her. "Sit down," she said, and sat down herself, facing Jo across her desk.

"Look, I'm sorry about this morning. It was just . . ." Jo's voice faded. It was just what? What could she say?

"You look really awful," said Miss McNeil. "Are you ill?"

"No, not ill," said Jo. "I mean I feel rough, but no, I'm not ill."

"What is it then? In class you looked as if your body was with us, but your mind was definitely somewhere else. Have you got problems? Family problems maybe? You can tell me if you have. Or is it the course work? Are you still finding it difficult to keep up? I have noticed an improvement lately."

Jo was close to tears, though she didn't want Miss McNeil to see that. "It's a bit of everything, I suppose. Relationships, work, you know. But not family problems — the only problem with my family is that they're a hundred miles away."

"So you're homesick?"

"No, not really. But I do miss my parents, my brother. I could talk things over with them, talk about anything that was bothering me. I miss that."

"Don't you have a close friend here? Lynn?"

"She's not really close, and anyway, she's got problems of her own. There's Nishma, and Andy Callaghan, you know, he's a third year . . . But, well . . ."

"They're not the same?"

"No, they're not. Look, I am sorry about this morning. You see, I didn't sleep well last night, and by the time I did drop off it was time to get up again. If Lynn hadn't woken me I'd probably be in bed still."

Miss McNeil stood up. "So you haven't eaten breakfast?"

"No, there wasn't time."

"I'll be back in a few minutes. Wait here," said Miss McNeil, and hurried out of her office.

She came back carrying a cup of tea and a slice of toast. "Eat that. You'll feel better."

Jo doubted that, but was surprised to find that she did feel slightly better after the tea and toast.

Miss McNeil had watched her eating, and spoke in a softer tone. "Look, I don't want to pry.

You're an adult now, and entitled to run your own life. But if you do have any problems you'd like to talk over . . . Well, I'm always here."

"Thanks," said Jo. She put down her cup and saucer. "But I think I'll try and work things out for myself. Relationship wise, anyway."

"And workwise?" said Miss McNeil. "Are you falling behind again?"

"A little. But I'll catch up. I suppose I'll have to cut down on my social life, see less of my boyfriend."

Miss McNeil nodded, but said nothing.

Jo paused. "There is one other thing," she said. "That special patient study you set. It's my patient, Nigel Weston. He's awful. He won't even speak to me, never mind co-operate on my project. Do I have to have him? Couldn't you give me someone else?"

"No."

"But he's impossible. He's rude and arrogant, and I just can't get through to him. I've tried, I really have."

"Then you'll have to try again."

"But I can't. I don't know what else to do."

"Think of something," said Miss McNeil. "You'll meet lots of patients who are far more difficult to deal with than Nigel Weston, let me tell you. It's up to you to stick at it, make contact. Remember patients are in a strange position in hospital – dependant, unsure, frightened. To many of them it's a really alien world – and to some of them nurses are the aliens."

"That's what he makes me feel like."

"Then it's up to you to change his views, isn't it? And what about later? You may be in charge of a ward full of Nigel Westons. They may be your responsibility. You won't be able to throw your hands up in the air then, and give up."

"I know, but . . ."

"No buts. Now I want you to give it another try. You've got a free period after the break, haven't you?" Jo nodded. "Go and talk to Nigel again. Don't think about it, just do it. All right?"

Jo nodded again. "All right."

Miss McNeil glanced at her watch. "Off you go then."

Jo was at the door when Miss McNeil spoke again. "And remember what I said, won't you? I'm always here if you need to talk. Okay?"

Jo nodded. "Yes. Thanks."

By the time Jo got to the canteen the others were on their way out. "Shall I wait for you?" said Lynn. "Are you coming back to the home?"

Jo looked brighter. "No, go on without me. I'm going to have another cup of tea – then I'm going to see Nigel Weston."

"Good. Good luck. See you later."

Jo found Nigel alone in the day room. He was

watching a low-budget Australian soap. "Hi!" Jo said as brightly as she could, sitting in the chair next to his. She nodded at the screen. "Any good?"

Nigel didn't take his eyes from the screen. "No."

Jo thought quickly. "I went to see that new Jack Nicholson movie the other night."

Nigel didn't move; his eyes were still glued to the screen.

"It was good. You'll have to try to get to see it when you get out of here."

Nothing.

Jo's lack of sleep was starting to give her a headache. "Look, Nigel, are you going to speak to me, or not?"

Nothing.

Jo was getting angry. "Look. I didn't choose to write this report on you, you know. No one in their right mind would choose to spend time with someone like you. You're rude and arrogant. What gives you the right to treat me like this? My whole future could depend on producing a good report, but how can I find out anything about you unless you talk to me? I've had warnings already — the next time I'll probably be thrown off the course."

Nothing.

Jo was shouting now. "But don't worry about

a small thing like that, Nigel, will you? Just sit there like a zombie, watching that trash and feeling sorry for yourself. You think you're being clever, don't you? Well, you're not, you're just being juvenile and stupid. I felt we might be friends, you know, but let me tell you, you don't deserve friends. You certainly don't deserve *me*. It's not my fault you're in hospital, you know." Jo jumped up and ran from the room, tears streaming down her face. "I hope you rot in here!"

That night Jo was sitting in the wine bar with Mark, as usual. But tonight the atmosphere between them was strained, uneasy. Jo felt shaky and upset — and it wasn't just through lack of sleep. She kept thinking back to her confrontation with Nigel, and of the awful things she'd said. She'd have to apologize. And she'd have to give up on him, tell Miss McNeil she just couldn't do the study. And where would that lead?

Mark took her hand. "Penny for them," he said gently.

"What?"

"Your thoughts, a penny for your thoughts. What's wrong? Jo, you've been miles away all night. I may as well not have been here."

"Sorry," said Jo. "I've got a lot on my mind,

that's all. The tutor gave me another in-depth interview this morning, and then I tried to make contact with Nigel Weston again. And failed."

"You shouldn't let it get to you."

"How can I help it?" said Jo. "It's my life, my career. I don't think you understand, Mark. I think Miss McNeil's not far from throwing me off the course. End of career."

Mark shrugged. "So? Would that be such a disaster? You don't seem to be enjoying the training that much. Is all the hard work worth it? The shifts, the pressures? And at the end of three years you won't earn any more than a shop assistant."

Jo was shocked. "Is that how you see it?" she asked. "Just in terms of an easy time, good money?" She didn't wait for an answer. "Well, I certainly don't. I've always wanted to be a nurse, and I still do."

"Well, all I know is that you wouldn't find me sticking it out in a job that made me so miserable, so unhappy," said Mark. "Come on, let's go."

Jo and Mark parted in silence outside the nurses' home. It was still only ten o'clock, and Jo found Nishma and Andy chatting in the kitchen.

"God, you look awful," said Andy.

"Thanks," said Jo. "I feel even worse than I look, if that's possible."

"Want to talk about it?"

Jo nodded and sat down.

Nishma gave Andy an 'I'll get out of here and leave you to it' look, and closed the door behind her, leaving them alone.

"What is it?" Andy asked. His heart ached to see Jo looking so forlorn, so hopeless, and he wanted to hold her, touch her. But he didn't; he knew that was the last thing she wanted from him. Friendship, yes, but more than that – no.

"What's wrong?" he asked quietly.

"Everything."

"Come on, that's a bit drastic. Is it the work, or this Mark bloke?"

"Work really, I suppose. You see, I've got this guy Nigel . . ."

"Mmm, Nishma told me. He sounds like hard work."

"Yeah, he is. But it's not just him. Mark wants me to be available all the time. He doesn't understand how much work I've got to do. McNeil's on my back. Oh, Andy, I'm wondering if it's all worthwhile."

"Nursing?"

"Yes. I failed so miserably with Nigel that I think it's really undermined my confidence; I just don't know if I've got what it takes to be a nurse."

"But surely you knew it would be hard? No one has ever said that nursing's an easy option. It isn't. But it is worthwhile and satisfying. I think it's a great job. And I think — no, I know — that you're going to be good at it."

"Maybe. Maybe not."

Andy's calm certainty about nursing made Jo feel more unsure than ever. He knew that he was doing the right thing for him, evidently, but suddenly Jo didn't feel so sure.

"Look, I'm going to bed. I need some sleep. And I mean really need it," she said. "See you tomorrow?"

"'Course. Goodnight, Jo — and stop worrying. It'll all come out right in the end."

"You sound like my horoscope."

"Do I? In that case I predict a happy ending." He stood up, then stopped. "Nearly forgot. One of the porters asked me to bring this across." He took a white envelope from his shirt pocket. "Some sort of a note."

Jo took the envelope and put it in her bag without looking at it. "It can wait," she said. "My eyes won't stay open long enough to read it. Goodnight, Andy."

"'Night."

CHAPTER TEN

CONTACT

Jo had fallen asleep as soon as her head touched the pillow, and when she woke up in the morning she felt as if she hadn't moved all night. She had slept deeply, and felt good. She felt rested, refreshed, and somehow more capable, able to face the day confidently.

She leapt out of bed, pulled the curtains open, then grabbed her washbag and towel and headed off for the shower room. She came back a few minutes later pink and glowing, her head wrapped in the towel. "Morning, Lynn. It's a lovely day, isn't it?"

This was quite a change in Jo's mood, and Lynn smiled. "You look very cheerful this morning," she said. "Any special reason?"

"Nope. None at all," said Jo, unwinding the towel and running her fingers through her damp hair. "I just feel good, that's all."

Lynn sat at the dressing table and started to

wipe cleanser from her face.

"No! I don't believe it. I just don't believe it!" said Jo, reading something in her lap.

Lynn glanced at Jo's image in the mirror. "Not another tall, dark stranger in those horoscopes of yours?" she asked.

"Not exactly," said Jo, looking up with a big grin on her face. "But it does concern a tall, dark stranger."

Lynn looked puzzled. "I'm sorry, you've lost me," she said.

Jo crossed the room and put a piece of paper into Lynn's hands. "Read that. Go on, just read that. Then tell me if I'm dreaming will you, if I'm imagining things?"

Lynn read the short note aloud. "Sorry I was such a wally. Come and see me again, will you? This time I'll talk to you – honest. Nigel." Lynn looked up. "Nigel Weston?"

Jo laughed, nodded her head. She took the note from Lynn and read it again. "So I'm not dreaming?"

"You're definitely not dreaming," said Lynn. "But I wonder what happened? I wonder why he's changed his mind?"

"I don't know," said Jo. "And I don't care. I just know that he'll agree to be my patient guinea-pig now. All is not lost."

Jo picked up her new copy of *Cosmopolitan* and

turned quickly to the horoscopes page. She smiled as she read. "I knew it," she said. "If you receive an unexpected invitation – go. That's what it says here. It must mean Nigel Weston. And it must mean that things are going to work out now. Oh, I just knew this was going to be a good day, I just knew it."

"So when are you going to see Nigel?"

"Lunch-time. I'll grab a sandwich and go over there. See what's brought about this sudden change of heart."

"Nigel?"

Jo stood by Nigel's bed, suddenly uncertain again. For a split second, a horrible thought flashed through her mind. The note! What if it was someone's idea of a joke? What if Nigel hadn't written to her after all? If this was a hoax, someone was going to pay dearly, and if that someone was . . .

Nigel turned and smiled, well, it was more of a grin, really. "Hi, Jo," he said.

This was such an about-turn from Nigel's usual attitude that Jo was floored, and suddenly didn't know what to say, even though she'd been rehearsing conversations in her head all morning. "Hi." She took the note from her pocket. "I got this. Did you send it?"

Nigel patted the bed. "Of course I did. Sit

down. I think I've got some explaining to do, haven't I? And an apology to make? I'm sorry I behaved the way I did, Jo, ignoring you like that. Forgive me?"

Was this the same Nigel Weston? Jo asked herself. Had he had a personality transplant in the last day or so? And what had brought about this change in him?

Jo was about to ask, when Nigel held up his hands. "Forgiven?" he asked.

"Yes, of course," said Jo. "But why . . ."

"Have you got all day? No, I'm sure you haven't, so I'll keep it short." He paused. "Come to think of it, I don't know if I can keep it short — because I don't know just where to begin."

"How about at the beginning?"

"Good idea, Nurse Carr," said Nigel. "Well, about three months ago — though it seems like three years ago sometimes — I borrowed a mate's bike, a big Kawasaki number, gleaming chrome, the lot. Took it out for a spin on the bypass, then a car overtook me, turned left in front of me without signalling or anything, I went over the handlebars — and the next thing I knew, I was in here. That's about it."

Jo knew all that from the patient records she'd been given. "But why wouldn't you . . ."

"Talk to you? That's a bit more complicated, though I think I'm beginning to understand it now. You see, when I came round I couldn't believe how badly injured I was. I sort of thought I'd have a few bruises, maybe a broken bone or two. But when I found I couldn't move my legs — wow! I couldn't accept it. I mean, the doctors told me I'd probably walk again okay, but it was that word probably that bugged me. What if I couldn't walk again? What if I had to spend the rest of my life in a wheelchair? I don't think you can imagine what it's like to live with something like that, the not knowing, the uncertainty."

"It must be devastating," said Jo. "But the outlook *is* good, isn't it?"

"Yeah, and looking better all the time," Nigel said. "It's just that being a long way from home, from my family and all my friends, I guess I just got really down lying here all day, every day. I mean, physiotherapy is murder, they really put you through it, but it got so that I looked forward to the sessions, just as a break from the awful monotony. Lying here all day I just got to imagining the worst."

"But why . . ."

"I know, I still haven't explained why I wouldn't speak to you. It sounds stupid, but I got to dread talking to anyone, even the staff here. I know they were all trying to help, but I got sick of hearing sympathetic voices, seeing concerned faces. They were all saying the same thing, you know, 'come on, it'll be all right, don't worry'. But I knew they were just trying to jolly me along, to cheer me up, and I didn't want to be wrapped in cottonwool, taken care of – I just wanted someone to tell me that my legs were going to work properly again. And of course that's the one thing they couldn't tell me for sure. It was okay them saying things would probably be all right, but I had to know for certain."

Jo nodded. "I can understand that. I think I'd feel really angry if I were you, trying to live with an uncertain future."

"You bet I was angry. I still am angry. Angry with the idiot who was driving the car, angry with the staff for not working miracles, angry with myself for reacting this way. So after weeks of listening to polite chat and sympathy, and getting angrier and angrier inside, you can imagine how I felt when you came along and wanted to do some sort of case study – with me as the case. I just decided I wasn't going to lie here making polite conversation anymore. And if I'm really honest, there's another reason. When you first came into the ward that day and I caught a glimpse of you, you reminded me of someone."

"Oh," said Jo. "A girlfriend?"

"Yeah, Helen. We've been going out together for months now, we're really close. But she lives back up north, and she can't get down here very often. I really miss her. And I suppose I'm scared that our relationship might not stand up to the strain of being separated, of not being able to see much of each other. Seeing you made me think of Helen again, and it just felt like another problem."

"But you still haven't told me why you changed your mind." Jo held up the note. "Why you sent this."

"Well, I suppose it was after you shouted at me in the day room. I was glad to hear an angry voice for a change. All the others have made allowances for my black moods, my rudeness. It was good to have someone shout at me for a change. And as I thought about it I realized how unfair I'd been to you. I think you were just at the wrong place at the wrong time, and I took all my frustration and anger out on you."

"I can understand that," said Jo. "I suppose if I'd been in your shoes I'd have felt the same. I wouldn't have liked answering lots of stupid questions, being some student nurse's guinea-pig." Jo stood up. "Anyway, I'm glad we've cleared the air. And thanks for the apology. Look, can I come and see you sometime — as a friend?"

Nigel grinned. "I'd like that. And next time, bring your clipboard and pen with you, okay?"

"You mean you're going to be my guinea-pig

– sorry, study patient – after all?"

"Yep." Nigel grinned again. "That is, if you still want me to be, and if you haven't found anyone else."

"I haven't found anyone else," said Jo, and looked at her watch. "It's five to. I've got to dash or I'll be in trouble. I'll come and see you tonight, okay?" She paused when she reached the door. "And keep it up."

"Keep what up?"

"Smiling. You're really quite good at it, you know."

Jo skipped along the corridor. She could still hear Nigel laughing as she went through the swing doors.

That night was just the first of many hours that Jo spent with Nigel over the next few weeks. Jo could hardly believe that this was the same Nigel. The old Nigel had been remote, rude, a real pain, if Jo was honest. The Nigel she came to know was funny, warm, interesting, and someone she really liked to spend time with. Jo made good progress with her special study report, but soon realized that she wasn't visiting Nigel just for the report's sake; she simply enjoyed being with him. They talked about everything and anything, and soon became important parts of each other's lives.

One day when Jo was heading for a lunch-time visit with Nigel, the unit sister called her into the office. "Can I speak to you?" she said.

For a split-second, Jo panicked. Was it bad news? Oh, no, not when Nigel had been making such good progress.

The sister smiled, and Jo relaxed slightly. "There's nothing wrong, is there?" she asked.

"No, nothing," said the sister. "Sit down. I just wanted to talk to you about Nigel."

"Yes?"

"I just wanted to thank you, really. I don't know if you realize it, but you've made a real difference to his life. You seem to have given him a more positive outlook, and that has borne fruit in his treatment. Things look very good for him now, you know. We think he'll make a good recovery, practically a full recovery."

"That's brilliant," said Jo, grinning from ear to ear. "Thanks for telling me. But I haven't really done anything practical, you know. We just talk. We're friends. I mean, I know I started visiting Nigel because he's my study patient, but now I come because I want to, not because I have to."

"I know. And don't underestimate the part you've played in Nigel's recovery. You've made him interested in life again, made him believe that he's going to get well. That's important in cases like his. We can give drugs, physio, offer support. But you've given Nigel something else – the will to fight. Don't underestimate that role; it's a very important one."

Jo felt a warm blush spread up her neck. "I won't," she said quietly.

Sister smiled. "I think you'll make a good nurse."

"Thanks," said Jo.

"Why don't you take Nigel outside for a while?" said the sister. "Get some fresh air? It's mild today."

Jo got up. "I will. And thanks again."

Jo found Nigel in the dayroom. "Hi, fancy a walk in the grounds?" said Jo. "Sister says it's okay."

Nigel picked up his two sticks and slowly got to his feet. "Great. Come on, race you to the bench."

Jo watched as Nigel walked slowly through the door. "Need any help?"

"No, but I'll let you give me a piggy-back ride back, okay?"

"You must be joking."

As they sat on the bench a few minutes later Nigel turned to Jo. "I saw you in Sister's office. You were talking about me, weren't you?"

"Yes, we were. And don't look so worried. It was all good news. You know you're getting better, don't you? The doctors are really pleased with the progress you're making. You just have to keep working at it."

"I know. If you'd told me I'd be walking again, even with sticks, a few weeks ago, I wouldn't have believed you. Yet here I am, mobile. It's just that I get really impatient sometimes. I want to be back to normal now, right away. It all seems so slow."

"Better slow than dead stop." Jo looked at her watch. "Oh, heck, it's ten to. Come on, we'll have to get back. I've got a physiology lecture with Miss McNeil at two."

"She still giving you a hard time?"

"Not too bad. But she still thinks I'm not working hard enough." Jo stood up. "Come on, move it! If you don't hurry I'll be late."

"Charming. What a way to talk to the patients. What would Miss McNeil say if she could hear you now?"

"I dread to think."

"Will I see you tonight? Or have you got work to do?"

"You know me," said Jo. "I've always got work to do. But all work and no play makes Jo a dull girl, so I'm taking a night off. Mark's taking me for a Chinese meal."

"Oh. So you won't be able to spare an hour for a poor, lonely patient?"

"No. And less of the poor and lonely. I've got

to finish my report on this Nigel Weston creep, then I'll meet Mark. I'll come tomorrow."

"Have you ever been hit with a walking stick?"

Jo ran off along the path. "You'll have to catch me first!"

Jo put down a spare rib and swished her fingers in the fingerbowl. "Well, I got my patient report finished. I'll hand it in tomorrow. I'm really pleased with it. I know it's good. Let's hope it keeps Miss McNeil happy."

"Mmmm."

"I suppose it's all down to Nigel really."

"Why? You did all the work didn't you? What's he got to do with it?"

"Lots. If he hadn't worked on it with me it wouldn't be nearly so good. I mean, you know what he was like when I first talked to him. Impossible."

Mark sucked on another spare rib. "Mmmm."

"And the study's optimistic, too. Nigel's going to make an almost full recovery. Sister told me today. That's great, isn't it? I mean I always hoped he would, thought he would, but now it's official. He probably won't be at St Stephen's much longer."

"That *is* good news."

"What do you mean?"

"Oh, it's just that you seem to be spending an

awful lot of time with this Nigel character. I mean, I know you had to talk to him to do this study thing, but you do seem to be taking it a bit far."

"A bit far? What are you talking about? You know Nigel's not just a patient anymore. He's a friend, a mate. We've grown quite close over the last few weeks."

Mark's face wore what was almost a sneer. "Quite close, eh? Tell me, Jo, just how close are you? What's going on between you and this cripple?"

Jo felt almost as if she'd been hit in the face. Cripple! How could Mark use that word – about Nigel? Jo was so shocked, so angry, that she couldn't speak. She just glared across the table at Mark as though he were a stranger.

"Well, just what is going on between you two?" Mark's voice was harsh, cold, insistent.

Jo locked the fingers of both hands together and squeezed until it hurt. She didn't know how else to control her anger, how else to stop herself exploding. She took a deep, deep breath, waited a second, then spoke in what she hoped sounded like a calm, controlled voice.

"Nigel is a friend. A good friend. There is nothing 'going on' between us. I don't know how you can even think that. And don't dare call Nigel a cripple. Don't call anyone a cripple.

How would you feel if someone called *you* that?"

Mark shrugged. His face looked grim. He didn't speak.

"Nigel's brave and funny and . . ."

"And fanciable?"

"I was going to say that he's kind . . . and witty. Perhaps you'd think that, too, if you'd ever taken the time to visit him with me. I've asked you often enough."

"You know how I feel about hospitals."

Jo screwed up her napkin and threw it on the table. "And about nurses, too, presumably."

She took her jacket from the back of the chair and walked out of the restaurant.

Mark didn't try to stop her . . .

Andy and Lynn were chatting over a frozen pizza when Jo walked into the kitchen. She didn't return their greetings, but went to the sink and poured a tumbler of water. She drank it, refilled the glass, and drank again. Then she pressed the cold glass surface against her forehead.

"You okay?" asked Andy. "What's wrong?"

All the way home Jo had felt hot tears pricking at her eyes, but she had held them back. Now, looking at the concerned faces of Lynn and Andy, she couldn't control them, and they spilled over her pale cheeks. She sobbed, and put her hands over her face.

Andy jumped up, put his arms around her, and held her tight. "Don't try to talk," he said. "Just let it all out."

Andy held Jo until her sobs slowly subsided. She fumbled for a paper tissue, blew her nose, and mumbled, "Sorry."

Andy released his hold on her. "Here, sit down. And when you can, tell us what happened."

Jo blew her nose again. "It's stupid really. I had a row with Mark, stormed out of the restaurant."

"Must have been serious for you to leave a Chinese meal uneaten."

Jo managed a weak smile. "I suppose it was. Mark accused me of fancying Nigel. Said we spent too much time together to be just friends."

"But he can't believe that, surely? I mean, you haven't kept your visits to Nigel secret, have you?"

"Of course not. I had no reason to. Sure, I like Nigel, we're great mates. But that's all. Oh, I can't believe Mark said those things."

"Well, if he doesn't trust you, maybe you're better off without him," Andy said quietly.

Jo started to sob again. "No, no, I can't imagine life without Mark. I love him. I love him!"

CHAPTER ELEVEN

MISERY

A black cloud of misery settled itself firmly over Jo's head for the next few days, and refused to be budged. Lynn, Nishma and Andy jollied, cajoled, sympathized and supported, but Jo remained sunk in gloom. She went around with a long face, jumped every time the phone rang, and spent most of the time in lectures staring into space or writing Mark's name over and over again in her notebook, like some lovesick first former. Without Mark her life seemed hopeless and empty. Even Nigel didn't seem able to reach her, and though she still visited him, there was a certain uneasiness between them now. Jo didn't like thinking it, but way at the back of her mind lurked the thought that if she hadn't spent so much time with Nigel, she'd still have Mark . . .

She wasn't proud of feeling like that, but no matter how often she told herself not to think of it in those terms, the idea just wouldn't quite go away. And though she hadn't told Nigel why she and Mark had argued, there was such a change in Jo's attitude that he suspected it was something to do with him. And that idea sunk him into gloom, too.

Jo couldn't even find any consolation in her horoscope predictions. In the mood she was in, even innocent warnings to avoid travel or new places became harbingers of disaster. Jo found herself looking at the world through a gloomy, grey cloud that she couldn't penetrate. Her mood was doomy and despondent.

When Jo was called into Miss McNeil's office for another pep talk, she accepted it with resignation; she'd expected a rocket after being pulled up so many times in the lecture room for daydreaming and not paying attention.

"Your patient study was excellent, really excellent," said Miss McNeil. "I really thought you'd turned the corner and were knuckling down to some hard work. But this week — well, I know your body has been with the rest of the class, but your mind certainly hasn't, has it?"

Jo saw no point in arguing; Miss McNeil was only stating facts, after all. "No. It's just that I've had problems . . . personal problems."

"With this boyfriend of yours?"

Jo sighed. "Ex-boyfriend. Yes."

"Oh." Miss McNeil paused, and shuffled some

papers on her desk. "Well, I'm sorry if things haven't worked out between you, but you can't let your work suffer. You have to leave your personal problems behind. Think about this boy as much as you like off-duty, but when you're on the wards or in lectures you must concentrate. It's vitally important. Remember, patients depend on you."

"I know. It's just that I can't get Mark out of my mind. I'm so unhappy, I just don't know what to do."

"I can't tell you what to do – no one can. I'm just telling you that you'll have to concentrate on your studies, or . . . It's your career, after all. Isn't it important to you?"

"Yes. It's just that I want Mark, too. I need him, I really do."

Miss McNeil was rapidly losing patience with Jo. "I suggest you take some time to decide your future. Have a good hard think about what's important to you."

"I will."

"Off you go now. And, Nurse Carr, I expect to see a real improvement in your attitude over the next few days."

She didn't actually say 'or else', but Jo felt that it was very much implied, and she left the office with those two words ringing inside her head. Jo wouldn't have thought it possible, but after the interview with the tutor, she felt even more down than before.

The next day was the first of Jo's two-day break, and she was determined to make good use of the time. She got up, showered and washed her hair, grabbed a mug of coffee, then went back to her room. She pinned a large 'do not disturb' sign to the door, and seated herself at the desk, a clean pad in front of her, a pile of textbooks at her elbow. She started to read, turned the pages, took notes – then found herself staring out of the window. Mark's face formed on the glass, and Jo found her thoughts turning to the good times they'd had together, how it had felt to be in Mark's arms, how his kisses had left her breathless and light-headed, how right it had all felt – how permanent. Tears fell down her cheeks, and she wiped them away almost angrily. Crying isn't going to help matters, she told herself. Mark's gone, finished and that's all there is to it, he's . . .

There was a soft knock on the door. "Jo, it's Nishma. There's . . ."

"Can't you read?" Jo shouted, trying to keep the tremble out of her voice. "Go away."

"But, Jo . . ."

"Go away, I said. Leave me alone!" Jo was shouting now, and when she heard Nishma walking away, she turned back to her books. But she couldn't read them — tears filled her eyes again, and this time there was no wiping them away, no holding them back. Jo put her face in her hands and let the tears flow . . .

Jo spent all day in her room. She worked, or tried to, blinking away the image of Mark's face when it materialized in front of the words she was supposed to be reading, trying to think about what was in the textbooks rather than what Mark might be doing. It wasn't easy, but Jo stuck at it, and when she finally straightened up and closed the books, she felt quietly satisfied. She'd worked hard, and had managed to catch up a lot of ground. Miss McNeil will be proud of you, she told herself.

Jo glanced at her watch. It was five o'clock, and she realized with a start that she felt hungry — very hungry. She turned off the anglepoise lamp, pulled a brush through her hair, and rushed into the kitchen.

Jo toasted some bread, warmed up a can of baked beans, and was just sitting down to eat when Nishma walked in.

"Hi," said Jo. "How's tricks?"

"Okay," said Nishma coolly, and Jo remembered how she'd shouted that morning.

"Sorry about this morning. I was trying to work. And I was in a foul mood. Friends again?"

"Sure," said Nishma, pouring a glass of milk

and sitting at the opposite side of the table.

Jo was about to put a forkful of beans to her mouth when she stopped halfway. She looked at a white envelope propped up against the teapot. "What's this?"

"It's what I was trying to tell you about this morning," said Nishma. "It came in the post. I thought you'd want to read it, but . . ."

Jo looked at the envelope. It was addressed to her. She ripped it open and took out a glossy card. On the front was a sad-looking rabbit carrying a huge bunch of flowers. Inside she read the short message: I'm sorry. Can you forgive me? I acted like the worst kind of fool. I still care, but do you? Love from Mark.

Jo kissed the card and rushed out into the hall, fumbling for change in her jeans pocket as she went. "I've got to catch Mark before he leaves work," she said, and said a silent prayer as the telephone rang out, first to the switchboard, then in Mark's office.

"Mark Laurence."

Jo's heart skipped a beat. "Mark? It's me – Jo. I just got your card. It came this morning but I was in my room, and then I said I didn't want . . ." The words came tumbling out. Jo had such a lot to say to Mark that she hardly knew where to begin.

When Jo paused for breath, Mark laughed. "Oh, Jo, it's so good to hear your voice again.

Are you free tonight? Yes? Great. I'll pick you up in an hour."

Jo was getting changed when she remembered Nigel. She pulled her jeans back on and sprinted over to the spinal unit. She burst into the ward with a cheesy grin on her face. "Guess what?" she cried. "He sent me a card to apologize. I think he wants us to get back together again. I'm seeing him tonight. That's why I came, to tell you I can't make visiting."

Nigel didn't seem to share Jo's joy. "It's okay," he said. "Have fun."

"But aren't you pleased for me? It's brilliant news, isn't it?"

"Yeah, I suppose so. If it's what you want."

"Of course it's what I want." No one was going to spoil Jo's mood, not even Nigel, she was determined about that. "Okay, be laid back and cool — see if I care." She turned and rushed out of the ward. "I'll try and get over tomorrow."

"Forgive me?" Mark looked deep into Jo's eyes. Their kiss had been long and intense, and they still held each other tightly, their lips an inch apart.

"Of course I do," said Jo. "It's forgotten now."

Mark released his grip on Jo's shoulders. "Shall we go to the wine bar?" he asked.

Jo shook her head. "I'd rather not. We're

bound to meet up with someone, and I want you all to myself. Let's walk down by the river."

They walked in silence for a while, then stopped and sat on a bench. Mark took Jo's hand in his. "I really am sorry, Jo. I acted like a prat. I was jealous of Nigel, I realize that now."

"But that's silly," said Jo. "He's a mate, that's all, like I kept telling you. You're my boyfriend — aren't you?"

Mark smiled. "If you'll have me back?"

"Idiot! Of course I'll have you back. I wish you'd never been away. I've been so miserable, Mark, you don't know."

"I think I do. Everything seemed empty without you. I missed you, I really did."

Mark took Jo in his arms and they kissed. Jo felt so happy she thought she would burst. She wished the kiss would go on forever. In Mark's arms was where she felt right, where she belonged.

They sat close together, Mark's arm around Jo's shoulders, and didn't speak for a while; words didn't seem necessary.

Then Mark sat up. "Nearly forgot. Tim's organized a weekend in the New Forest. His aunt owns this big country place that she rents out, and he's got good rates for a weekend. I asked him to keep two places for us. You'll come with me, won't you?"

Jo smiled. "You asked him to keep places for us, did you? So you were pretty confident that we'd get back together?"

"I hoped we would. Will you come?"

"Of course I'll come. When is it?"

"Next weekend. We leave on Friday night, come back Sunday night."

Jo counted on her fingers. "Five days on, two days off. That takes us to . . . Oh, Mark, I have to work this Saturday."

"Can't you change with someone? This is special, you can't miss it."

"No, I can't. But we could drive down on Saturday, couldn't we? I finish just after four."

Mark's face looked grim. "I'm not driving all the way down there for one night," he said. "It's just not worth it."

"But Mark, why not? I mean, what can I do?"

"Can't you sneak off or something? Tell them you've got to go to a funeral or something?"

"I can't just sneak off. I'm on the wards. People will be depending on me. I know I'm a lowly student, but if I'm not there it will make heaps more work for everyone else."

Mark was insistent. "But it's only for one day, Jo. Tell them you're ill. That's it, tell them you've got a tummy bug or something. They'll believe you, won't they?"

"I'm sure they will, but . . ."

Mark took Jo's hands in his and squeezed them hard. "Then do it, Jo, do it. For me. For us. We need the time together."

"I know we do. But I just don't know if . . ."

"Do it, Jo. I really want you to come with us, you know I do."

Jo took a sharp intake of breath. She spoke quietly. "You mean you're going anyway? You mean you'll go there without me if I can't get the time off?"

"Well, it's booked . . . But, Jo, say you'll come. Please?"

So, thought Jo, he'll go whether I do or not. At least I know exactly where I stand. "So I have no choice, really, do I?" she said. "If I want you, I have to fit in with your plans. It's almost as if you're asking me to choose between you and my career."

"That's a bit too simplistic. I just want you with me."

"And I want you with me. But nursing's important, too. I can't just drop everything when you tell me to. Nursing *is* different, Mark. It makes demands on people. I'm trying to accept that it makes demands on me, asks questions of me. But you don't seem to accept that."

"I just think it's a job, not a whole way of life. It shouldn't dictate your whole life."

Jo stared straight ahead. "I see."

Mark didn't seem to notice her mood. "So you'll come, Jo? You'll tell them you're ill? It's only for one day."

Jo stood up. "Come on, let's go back. I'm getting cold."

She walked ahead and Mark ran after her. He caught her, spun her round, and kissed her lightly. "So you'll come?"

Jo looked into Mark's dark eyes and felt her resolve draining away. But she wouldn't commit herself. "I'll think about it."

CHAPTER TWELVE

ANDY

Jo wouldn't go to the wine bar with Mark. She said she was tired, and needed an early night, but she really needed to think, to talk, to make decisions.

She said goodbye to Mark, then she walked across to the hospital's main entrance and sat down on the steps. She knew Andy would be coming off duty at nine . . .

"Hello. What are you doing here?" Jo turned to face Andy, and smiled.

"Came to see you. Can we talk? I need some advice." She looked at Andy's face. He looked tired, maybe a little pale. "Or are you too tired?"

"No. But what's wrong? Have you crossed swords with Miss McNeil again?"

"I'll tell you later," said Jo. "Come back to the nurses' home, huh? If I want to pick your brains, at least I can feed you first. How about a special Carr cheese omelette?"

"Sounds good, Come on. You get frying, and I'll get a bottle of wine from the off licence."

Jo and Andy were sitting at the table half an hour later. Andy poured out second glasses of wine. "Well, I feel human again now. Thanks, Jo. Now what's the problem? What do you need to talk about?"

"Mark."

"Oh, him."

"And me. And nursing. And my future."

"This sounds ominous. Why not start at the beginning?"

Jo did just that. She told Andy about the row, how Mark had sent the card by way of an apology, and about his plans for the New Forest weekend. "But I'm on duty on Saturday. Mark thinks I should say I'm ill. Go on the weekend anyway."

Andy stared into his wine glass. "And you're tempted to go along with it?"

"If I'm honest, yes, I am tempted. I realize it's wrong, that I shouldn't even be thinking of doing it – but yes, I'm tempted."

"Mark means that much to you, then?" asked Andy.

"That's what I've got to decide. It seems he's almost asking me to choose – him or nursing."

"But you shouldn't have to make a choice like that. Nursing's your career, a career you've just started. Surely you can't think of giving it up for a bloke you've only known for a couple of months?"

Jo sighed. "I am thinking about it. I feel I'm being forced to. You see, nursing isn't my whole life. I'm not totally dedicated, like Lynn. I mean, some people say you have to have a real vocation to nurse. But I don't think I have a vocation. I can't have, can I, if I'm thinking about pretending illness to get off duty?"

Andy looked up. "Don't be too hard on yourself. So you haven't got a vocation. Neither have I. I just enjoy nursing. The fact that it's worthwhile is secondary. I do it because it's what I want to do."

"But I'm not one hundred per cent sure any more. I don't know if I have the determination to make it."

"But what if you give up? You'll have to do something else. And what if you and Mark don't stay together? What then? You'll have given up a good career for nothing."

"I suppose so, but . . ."

"And what about Mark? I don't think much of him if he asks you to give up nursing just to fit in better with his social life. He sounds really possessive, as if he wants your life to revolve around him. And just because nursing can be a bit hard on his social life, he expects you to give up."

"I know. But I don't want to lose him."

Andy and Jo talked on, long after the bottle of wine was finished. The others came and went, then the quiet of early morning came down. Still they talked, now over mugs of hot chocolate.

And that was how Miss McNeil found them. "I thought I heard voices in here," she said. "What are you doing here, Nurse Callaghan? It's nearly two o'clock in the morning. You know you shouldn't be here after eleven."

"Sorry," said Andy. "I suppose I just forgot the time."

Jo stood up. "It's not his fault. I asked him to come. I needed someone to talk to. I . . ."

"I suggest you leave now, Nurse Callaghan," said Miss McNeil coldly. "You're a third year. You know the rules. See me in the morning before you go on duty."

Andy picked up his jacket. "Yes, I will. Goodnight, Jo."

"Goodnight," said Jo. "But look, Miss McNeil, it wasn't Andy's fault, he only . . ."

But Miss McNeil wasn't listening; she had turned and was walking down the corridor.

Jo blew out a long, long breath of air, then stood up and snapped off the light. She threw herself into bed minutes later and was asleep almost before her head hit the pillow.

Lynn was on early shift, and when Jo woke up the room was quiet and empty. The memories of last night surfaced immediately and she groaned. She still had to decide what to do about the weekend with Mark – and now she'd managed to get Andy in trouble.

Jo jumped out of bed. She felt angry on Andy's behalf, and dressed quickly. "Miss McNeil had no right to react like that," she said under her breath. "She didn't even listen when I tried to explain. But I'll *make* her listen."

Jo marched across to Miss McNeil's office without stopping for breakfast. She knocked sharply, and flung open the door as soon as she heard, "Come in."

"I've come about Andy, about what happened last night. You had no right to speak to him like that. It wasn't . . ."

"Nurse Carr!" Miss McNeil's voice was strong and firm, and stopped Jo in her tracks. "That's enough! Now, if you'd like to sit down and talk about this sensibly, please do. If not, you can leave my office right now."

Jo felt a pink blush form on her cheeks, and realized how rude she must have sounded. She put her hand to her face, flustered and uncertain. "Sorry," she mumbled.

"Sit down," said Miss McNeil, and when Jo had sat in silence for a few seconds, she looked up. "What do you have to say for yourself?"

Jo took a breath. "Well, I just wanted to talk to you about last night. About Andy, Nurse Callaghan, being in the nurses' home. I mean, I know it was well after hours, but surely it's not such a big deal? And it was my fault. I asked him to come over. I needed someone to talk to."

"But Nurse Callaghan knows the rules."

Jo was exasperated, but tried to keep the annoyance out of her voice. "Yes, I know he does. But I really needed to talk to him, and the time just flew by. We didn't set out to sit there until the early hours. Andy had just come off late shift, and he must have been shattered. But I desperately needed to talk to him, to get his advice about something."

"About what?"

Jo didn't want to tell Miss McNeil about Mark. "Oh, just a personal problem." She decided to try and make light of it, to stop Miss McNeil asking awkward questions; questions that she knew she wouldn't want to answer. "It was nothing really, nothing important."

"Then why did you need to talk to him so desperately? Surely it could have waited?" said Miss McNeil coolly.

"Well, it was important, and I did want Andy's advice, but . . . Look, I just think you're being unfair, blaming him. You mustn't discipline him.

It wasn't his fault. It's just not fair. Take it out on me; it was my fault. If I hadn't asked for his help he wouldn't be in trouble . . ."

Jo was angry now, angry and upset. She felt hot, and her stomach lurched up under her ribs. Her face burned, and she felt panicky. "It's not Andy's fault!" she managed to blurt out, before her shoulders were racked with heaving sobs, and tears started to course down her face. Breaking down in front of Miss McNeil was the last thing she'd intended doing – but she had been powerless to stop herself.

Miss McNeil sat quietly as Jo cried, then as the sobs subsided slightly, she handed over a paper tissue. "Now, are you going to tell me what's bothering you? It's evidently something import-ant, or you wouldn't be in this state. Come on, Nurse Carr, tell me. It might surprise you, but I'm quite a good listener. Come on, blow your nose and dry your eyes."

Jo realized that there was no point in denying that she had problems. She'd never been a weepy type of girl, but now she seemed to be making a regular thing of bursting into tears. Maybe Miss McNeil could help. At least she was prepared to listen. "I wanted to talk to Andy about my future. I just don't know what to do. I just don't know where I'm heading. I'm really mixed up."

"You said it was a personal problem. Does it

concern this boyfriend of yours?"

"Yes. We were really serious about each other, then we split up. I was really upset. Then he sent me a card to say sorry, and I thought we were back together. But he doesn't understand about nursing, about the course, about shifts. He can't accept that I don't do a nine to five job, that I can't always see him just when he wants me to."

"But surely you can explain? Surely he would make allowances?" said Miss McNeil.

"I've tried, I really have. But he just has the attitude of 'why do it if it interferes with your life so much?' He says he works to live, not lives to work."

Miss McNeil's brows furrowed. "This young man seems to take a rather simplistic view of life. Nurses aren't hermits. We all have a life outside the job. It's just that patients aren't just ill between the hours of nine to five. Have you explained all this to him?"

Jo sighed. "I've tried. But it's difficult. And now he wants me to go away for the weekend with him. When I explained that I couldn't go until Saturday, he said I should go anyway, say I'm ill, and not fit to work."

"I see. And is this what you wanted to talk to Nurse Callaghan about? Were you thinking of saying you were ill and going?"

Jo shrugged. "I know it's wrong, I know it is. But you see, Mark says he'll go on the weekend whether I'm with him or not. He won't make allowances. It's almost as if he's asking me to choose between nursing and him."

"And?"

"And right now I just don't think I can make that choice. It isn't fair. I just don't know what to do. I don't want to give up nursing — but I don't think I can be a nurse and Mark's girl as well. And I love Mark."

"I see."

Jo sighed. "That's what I wanted to talk to Andy about. We're good friends, and I care about what he thinks. I wanted to talk things through with him. That's why he was with me last night."

"I understand. I think you've got some big decisions to make, Josephine. I don't think you should have to make them — but there we are. I think you need to take some time off. Go home for a couple of days. Get away from St Stephen's — and from this boyfriend of yours."

"But my work . . . . the wards. I'm on duty . . ."

"I'll take care of that," said Miss McNeil firmly. "Forget St Stephen's for a day or two. Think hard about your future. What you decide could affect the rest of your life, remember."

"I know," said Jo miserably.

"Go back and pack right away. Ring home, tell them you're on your way. Then just catch the first bus. Okay?"

Jo felt strangely relieved. The thought of going home hadn't occurred to her; she hadn't thought it possible. But now that Miss McNeil had made it almost an order she realized how glad she would be to go home, to think, to talk. She nodded. "Okay. And thanks, Miss McNeil. You've been very understanding."

Miss McNeil smiled. "I try to be, though it's not always easy. Now go home, and sort yourself out. And I hope you make the right decision."

"So do I," said Jo, her hand on the door handle. "So do I."

Just as Jo was about to close the door behind her, Miss McNeil spoke again. "Oh, and Nurse Carr, don't worry about Nurse Callaghan. I won't be disciplining him, just having a chat. And I think he can take care of himself, you know."

"Thanks," said Jo, and thought to herself, yes, I know he can. He certainly wouldn't get himself into a mess like this, that's for sure.

Jo packed a small grip, then wrote out a short note and put it on the desk, propped up against the lamp: Gone home for a couple of days to sort myself out. I've got some thinking to do, some

decisions to make. See you soon. Jo. Then she left
the nurses' home and headed for the bus station
in town, without giving St Stephen's a backward
glance . . .

CHAPTER THIRTEEN

HOME

The front door opened almost as soon as Jo turned her key in the lock. Standing in the hall was Tim, her brother. He looked worried and concerned. "Jo? Are you all right? Is there anything wrong? I mean, this is an unscheduled trip, isn't it? We weren't expecting to see you for weeks. Are you ill or something?"

Though Jo had spoken to Tim on the phone to tell him she was going home, she hadn't gone into details; she felt there'd be plenty of time. Anyway, she wanted to talk to Tim and her parents face to face, not over the telephone. "Don't panic," she said now. "I'm fine. I just got a couple of days leave to come home. There are things I need to talk to you about, things I need to decide about."

"Oh," said Tim, taking Jo's grip and putting it at the bottom of the stairs. "Come on, the coffee machine's been on for ages."

"Mmm," said Jo, sitting at the so-familiar kitchen table, "real coffee. We usually have instant, but it's just not the same, is it?"

Tim sat down opposite his kid sister. Even though Jo had said she was okay, he still looked concerned. Jo's face was paler than usual, and her eyes didn't seem to have their usual sparkle. "Do you want to talk now, or wait until Dad gets home?"

"It'll keep," said Jo. "I think I'll have a long bath, then maybe we'll talk after dinner, yes? But where's Mum? She should be home by now, surely?"

"Have you forgotten? She's away on a course this week. She's hoping she'll be made a supervisor if she does well."

"Of course," said Jo, though she'd completely forgotten about the course her mum had been so excited about. "Damn. I meant to ring her before she left, to wish her luck. Oh well."

"You could always ring her at the hotel. I've got the number."

"No. I'll see her the next time I'm home. She'll have enough to do on the course, without worrying about me. Look, if she rings, don't tell her I'm here, all right? Tell her when she comes home. She'll panic if she thinks she's not here to help."

"Okay, if that's what you want," said Tim.

"Why don't you unpack your things while I run a bath for you?"

Jo smiled happily. "Is this really my brother speaking? Taking my bag, running a bath for me? What's got into you?"

"Dunno. It's just you sounded so upset on the phone – and you look awful."

Jo laughed out loud. "Thanks a bunch! You really know how to make a girl feel good. But seriously, don't worry about me. I've just got a decision to make. It's a big one, and I couldn't think of a better place to make it than here. Or a better person to talk it over with than you. Now will you go and run that bath for me?"

Tim jumped up. "I'm on my way."

As he bounded up the stairs two at a time, Jo went out into the hall. "Tim," she called. "Don't forget the bubble bath, will you?"

When Jo came downstairs two hours later she felt and looked much better. She had bathed, washed her hair, then pottered around her room in a dressing gown before getting dressed. It had felt good, reassuring almost, to lie on the bed that had always been hers, to handle the old dolls and toys that still filled a cupboard, to laugh at the long-forgotten pop star faces that still looked down from posters on the wall. Apart from the room being tidy and neat, it looked just as it had done when she'd moved to St Stephen's months before.

She had heard her father's car drive into the garage, and had given Tim a couple of minutes to break the news of her unscheduled appearance before going downstairs.

Jo's dad was waiting at the bottom of the stairs. He gave her a big bear hug, then held her at arm's length. "Hello, love. My, it's good to see you. How's the course going? When do they make you Matron?"

"It's good to see you too, Dad. Things are okay. And we don't have matrons any more."

"Oh well, if they did, I'm sure you'd be one, right?" Mr Carr put his arm around Jo's shoulders. "Come on, let's eat."

Jo's dad didn't lead her into the kitchen, as she had expected, but into the dining room. The table was set with the best china and cutlery, and two tall candles burned in the centre. "Wow," said Jo. "What's the occasion?"

"My favourite sister coming home, that's what," said Tim, carrying in a tureen of soup.

"Your *only* sister," said Jo. "But when did you do all this?"

Mr Carr laughed. "He didn't. Your mum left a freezer full of food. There's enough stuff in there to last a month, never mind four days. I told her we wouldn't starve, but you know your mother."

Jo and her family chatted through the meal. It felt really good to Jo to be home again, with the familiar comfortable house and the equally comfortable faces of the people she loved. She was able to almost forget just why she was here, but not quite. Disturbing images of Mark and St Stephen's kept surfacing in her mind, no matter how hard she tried to keep them out.

It was as they sat on at the table after the meal was finished that Mr Carr cleared his throat and looked intently at Jo. "Well, love, Tim tells me there's something you want to talk to us about. What is it?"

That's Dad, thought Jo, direct as ever. She picked up the peppermill from the table and turned it in her fingers. Then she looked up, first at her father, then at Tim. "Phew. Now I'm here I don't really know where to begin."

"At the beginning," said her father. "Come on now, Jo, you've never been one for being short of something to say."

Jo laughed. "No, I suppose not." She took a deep breath. "Right, here goes. I've got to decide whether to carry on at St Stephen's or not. Whether I still want to be a nurse."

"But what's brought this on?" said Mr Carr. "You've always wanted to be a nurse, ever since you were a little girl."

"I know, Dad, but now . . ."

"Is it the classroom work? Are you finding it difficult? Surely you can get help? Or is it something that's happened on the wards? Has something upset you?"

"No, Dad, it's nothing like that." Jo looked at her father's concerned face, and wanted to reassure him. "No, I'm thinking of leaving because I've met a boy. I told you about him — Mark? He doesn't like me being a nurse, and the shifts and things are making it difficult for me to see him when he wants me to. I think what it comes down to is that I've got to choose between nursing and him."

Tim's face wore a puzzled expression. "But why? Surely you can be a nurse *and* have a boyfriend? Thousands of people do."

"Yes, I know," said Jo. "But Mark — well, he just doesn't understand. He won't make allowances. I think if I stay on at St Stephen's I'll lose him."

"But we didn't know it was so serious between you and this Mark boy. I mean, you've never brought him home or anything, and you haven't known him that long, have you? I mean, it's not as if you're planning to get married or anything." Mr Carr's eyebrows raised to form a question. "Are you?"

"No. But the very fact that he's made me think of giving up nursing means I'm not very dedicated, doesn't it?"

"It means nothing of the sort!" her father said sternly. "I think this boy's unsettled you, my girl, that's all. You think about it. Think hard. Is it worth giving up a career you've always wanted for this boy?"

Jo shrugged. "That's what I don't know, Dad. That's what I've got to decide."

Later that night Jo lay sprawled on her bed while Tim lay on the sheepskin rug beside it. Jo had talked and talked about her life at St Stephen's, about Mark, Andy, Nigel, Lynn and the others. But still she came back to the central problem — was she going to carry on with her nursing training or not? "I don't know what to do," she said. "I feel really mixed up and uncertain."

Tim had no such doubts. "Well, if you want my opinion, I think you'd be a real wally to give everything up. You worked hard to get a place at St Stephen's and you've not even finished your first year. And as for this Mark guy — sorry, but he must have hidden virtues or something, because he sounds like a real dead-loss to me. If he cared about you — really cared — he wouldn't expect you to give up your career just to be at his beck and call. This is the nineteen nineties, you know, not the eighteen nineties — women can be seen *and* heard now; I shouldn't have to tell you that. He sounds like a selfish and immature bloke, if you want my opinion."

For Tim this was a long speech, and Jo was surprised at his vehemence. She must have painted an awful picture of Mark. "But Mark hasn't told me to give up, you know," she said, feeling forced to defend him. "I just feel I'll have to choose between him and nursing sooner or later."

"But you shouldn't have to," said Tim. "And I'm sorry, Jo, but he sounds a dead-loss — superficial and shallow. You deserve someone better — someone like this guy Andy."

Jo's eyes opened wide. "Andy?" she said. "What do you mean? Andy's a friend, that's all, a mate."

"Maybe," said Tim. "But he seems to be the person whose opinions you respect. He seems to be the one you confide in. You care what he thinks, don't you? Really care. I mean, you talk to Andy, don't you, really talk to him about important things, not just about what new CD you're going to buy, what clothes are in this week. And Andy must care about you. Think about it."

"But Mark's my boyfriend. And he just doesn't understand about nursing."

"But why doesn't he? It's a part of your life. It's a big part of what you are. I mean, what do you see in Mark?"

"Well, he's fun, and witty, and I enjoy being with him. We go out all the time, to parties, and discos, and . . ." Jo's voice trailed off as Tim looked hard at her. It sounded superficial and unimportant. Jo realized with a real shock that Tim's question was almost impossible for her to answer. What did she see in him? What made her believe she loved him?

Tim shook his head. "I'm not the world's greatest lover, not even an expert on being in love," he said quietly. "But I do know that loving someone's not just about having a flash social life, being seen as a smart couple in all the trendiest places. It's about respect, caring, support – things like that."

Jo's voice was hardly louder than a whisper. "I know," she said. "But thanks for reminding me."

Tim stood up. "It's late. I think we both need some sleep."

He went to the door, then paused. "Have you decided what to do yet, Sis?"

Jo looked up and smiled. "No, not yet. But I'm getting there. Goodnight, Tim – and thanks."

"No sweat," said Tim. "Goodnight, Jo."

When Jo woke up early next morning she was surprised to realize that she felt good, rested, and not nearly so nervous and uncertain. She got dressed, went downstairs, and had a cooked breakfast ready for her dad by eight o'clock.

"You're spoiling me," said Mr Carr. "Just like your mother."

Jo smiled.

"What's the plan for today?" asked Mr Carr.

"There isn't one really. I'm just going to laze around. Do some more thinking, I suppose."

"When do you have to be back at the hospital?"

"Miss McNeil – that's my nurse tutor – wasn't specific. But I can't stay too long. It wouldn't really be fair."

"But you'll still be here when I get in from work?"

"Yeah, sure. So will Tim. He's ringing work to let them know that he's taking the day off. I told him he didn't have to, but . . ." Jo shrugged.

"He wants to help, love," said Mr Carr. "He cares a lot about you, you know that."

"Yes, I know he does."

"And so do we, your mum and me. Whatever you decide, we'll support you. No criticism, no arguments. It's your life, but . . ."

"But what?" said Jo.

"Well, we're proud of you, you know that, but I must admit I've been extra proud to be able to tell people that my daughter's a nurse. There's something special about that."

"Yes," said Jo, and decided it was time to

change the subject. "It's half past, Dad, you're
going to be late."

Mr Carr put on his jacket and kissed the top of
Jo's head, ruffling her hair in just the way that Jo
remembered him doing when she was a little girl.
"See you tonight."

"Bye, Dad."

That afternoon, Jo, Tim and their dog, Bosun,
went for a walk in the park. Tim had offered Jo
lunch, and had asked if she wanted to look up
some of her friends, but Jo had refused. "I'm here
to think," she'd said. "If I see people they'll only
ask why I'm here, and I don't want to go through
it all again. Anyway, I value your opinions more
than anyone else's."

"Do you?"

"Of course I do. You probably know me better
than anyone else does."

They sat on a bench and Bosun snuffled in the
undergrowth around the pond. "I don't know if I
do. I mean, I don't think there's any decision to
make. This Mark sounds selfish. He seems to put
himself first, sees things in terms of how they
affect him, just him. He seems to treat you as
some sort of accessory or something. I mean,
relationships are about being partners, about
sharing, aren't they? But because his job is nine to
five and yours isn't, he wants you to give up."

"He hasn't actually asked me to leave the hospital," said Jo. "It's just that I feel under pressure to fit in with him, be available. And I think that if I don't go away with him this weekend, he'll go anyway."

"So he's pressuring you, forcing you to choose. I know which I'd choose, Jo, no doubts. I don't think you've got a future with Mark, but I do think you've got a future with nursing. And you must have a future with someone who accepts both you and your career. It is a part of you, after all."

"Yes, I know."

"And what will you do if you leave St Stephen's? You've always wanted to be a nurse. I should know – I used to be your patient, didn't I? I seem to remember I spent quite a lot of time being bandaged and dosed with medicine."

"I don't know. Maybe get a job in a shop, take a typing course . . ."

"You sound very enthusiastic about that, I don't think!" said Tim. He glanced at his watch. "Come on, Jo, Bosun, let's get back. I have some heavy defrosting to do. Ah, a host's work is never done . . ."

That night over dinner Jo vetoed any further talk about Mark and St Stephen's. As they sat over coffee Jo said, "I'm going back tomorrow morning."

"So you've decided what to do?" asked Mr Carr.

"Well, I think I have," said Jo. "I'm almost certain that I'm going to carry on with my training — if they'll have me."

"Brilliant!" said Tim. "But what about Mark?"

"Well, I know you don't think much of him; I must have painted a very black picture of him. But I still care about him." Jo pushed her coffee cup away. "I'll just have to see what happens, won't I? Either he wants me for me — nursing, warts and all — or he doesn't."

"If he cares he'll make allowances for the job, Jo," said her father. "If he's good enough for you — which I very much doubt — he won't care if you're a coalman or a roadsweeper."

Jo could only hope that what her father had said would turn out to be true. But she had her doubts . . .

CHAPTER FOURTEEN

DECISION

All the way back to St Stephen's on the bus, Jo stared glassily out of the window. Though she had made her decision, she was still riddled with doubts: she didn't want to give up nursing, she knew that now – but she didn't want to lose Mark, either. Oh, why couldn't she have both? But she realized that to achieve that, Mark would have to change, to make fewer demands on her time. If he didn't, Jo's work would suffer again – and then the decision about being a nurse might be taken out of her hands altogether; she might be thrown off the course. Jo tried to summon up a resolve she wasn't sure she had, to tell herself that she wasn't going to fail, wouldn't be forced to give up. She thought of her father's words – 'if he cares he'll make allowances' – but the 'if' was a big one.

When she walked into the room she shared with Lynn, she was surprised to find that she was glad to be back; amazingly, it was starting to feel like home. Equally amazingly, the room looked a mess — and Jo was startled to realize that the clothes and books strewn around were Lynn's, not hers.

Lynn was using a hotbrush on her hair, but unplugged the brush as soon as Jo came in. "Oh, Jo, I'm so glad to see you. I've been so worried about you. Your note didn't say much, and Miss McNeil wouldn't tell me much more." She put a hand on each of Jo's arms and squeezed firmly. "Are you all right, Jo?"

Jo was a little taken aback. She'd never thought of Lynn as a close friend, just as a room-mate; and at the start she felt she'd been somewhat lumbered with Lynn. Chalk and cheese, they were. Lynn neat and tidy and meticulous in knuckling down to work and studying; Jo untidy, disorganized and wanting to work and play. But she realized suddenly that she was really glad to see Lynn again, wanted to talk to her. Lynn looked really concerned, and Jo decided there and then that she would help, be supportive. Without either girl realizing it fully, their uneasy alliance had become a real friendship.

Jo smiled at her. "Can we talk? And have you got all day?"

Lynn nodded. "I'm on lates."

Jo told Lynn about Mark, and the weekend invitation, and Andy being found in the kitchen by Miss McNeil, and how she'd gone to see Miss McNeil, and been sent home to sort herself out.

"And have you sorted yourself out?" Lynn asked. "Oh, don't say you're going to leave, Jo, please don't. I'd really miss you – we all would. And you're such a good nurse, you must realise that. Some of us find the whole thing hard, theory *and* practice. But you – you get on so well with the patients, put them at ease, let them see you really care. And that's more than half what it's all about, isn't it – tender loving care?"

Jo had never thought of herself as a good nurse, but it gave her a curiously warm, satisfying feeling to hear that Lynn thought of her in those terms. And Jo could see that she meant it, every word. "I've decided to carry on," said Jo, "and hope that Mark understands. If he doesn't . . ." Jo left the sentence unfinished.

"Thank goodness," said Lynn. "Oh, I'm so glad. We've all been worried, Jo – Andy more than anyone. He's been here more than in his own flat, I think."

Tim's words flashed into Jo's mind: 'Andy must care about you. Think about it'. She did, and a sudden realization hit her with a rush: she cared a lot about Andy, really cared. She hadn't thought of it before, but suddenly knew just how much she would miss him if she weren't at St Stephen's. In her time at St Stephen's he'd become very important to her; just as important, perhaps, as Mark . . . Maybe Andy and Mark were important to her for different reasons, but . . .

Jo shook herself mentally. One thing at a time, she told herself, one thing at a time.

She looked around. "What time is it?" she asked. "Where's your Mickey Mouse clock?"

Lynn rummaged in a messy pile of dirty washing that was strewn over the floor by her bed. "It must be here somewhere," she said. "I had it this morning, I'm sure I did." She found the clock eventually, half hidden in a sock. "It's half past two."

Jo sounded resolved. "Right. That gives me time for a shower before I go to tell Miss McNeil what I've decided. I'll catch her at break time." She looked around. "Have you seem my bath robe? It was on my bed, I think."

Jo searched for the robe without success. She looked around the room, then at Lynn. "Hey, what's happened in here? This place is a real mess. Now if you'd gone home and I'd been here on my own for two days, I could understand it looking like this, but you? You're usually so neat and tidy."

"Oh, yes, it is a bit of a mess, isn't it?" said Lynn.

"I hadn't really noticed. I've been . . . well . . . busy."

Jo laughed out loud. "What?" she cried. "Hey, what's been happening since I went home?"

A soft pink blush appeared on Lynn's cheeks. "Well, it started before you went home, actually. I suppose you just didn't notice . . ."

"But what happened?"

"Well, you know the junior registrar, Rob Swann?"

Jo nodded. "The Incredible Hunk, as Nishma calls him? Of course I know him. Every female in this hospital knows him — or would like to."

"Well, he, I mean, we . . ."

Realization dawned. "You mean you and Rob Swann? You're going out with him?" Jo asked.

"Mmmm," said Lynn, smiling happily. "It's been five, no, six days now. I've seen him every night."

"Well, you're a dark horse, Lynn Brooking. Fancy you landing a catch like him. And I don't have to ask if you like him — your face says it all. Well, well!"

Jo was still smiling as she groped under her bed, finally emerging with the bath robe. She went to the door, then paused. "Aren't you on duty soon, Lynn?" she asked.

"God, yes, I'd better hurry," said Lynn. "Where's my cap?"

"I don't know — but your heart's on your sleeve!" called Jo, and she laughed as a well-aimed pillow hit the back of the door behind her. "See you later."

Jo dressed in her uniform and waited in the corridor until she saw Miss McNeil heading for her office. "Hello, Nurse Carr," said the tutor. "Come in."

Jo felt hesitant and nervous. She decided to get this interview over with as soon as possible. "I've decided to stay — if you'll have me," said Jo quickly. "And I've decided to work harder, make more effort."

Miss McNeil smiled warmly. "I'm really glad, Josephine," she said. "I know you've made the right decision. And your boyfriend?"

"I don't know. I suppose he either accepts me, nursing and all — or he doesn't."

"Good. So you'll be back on duty tomorrow?"

"I'm ready now, if you need me," said Jo, who really wanted to get back to work.

"No, take the rest of the day off," said Miss McNeil. "See you tomorrow."

"Yes," said Jo. "And thanks, Miss McNeil, thanks for your help. You've been very understanding."

"It's all part of the job," said the tutor, but Jo noticed that she looked pleased, as if she really couldn't help smiling, even though she tried to look businesslike.

Outside the office, Jo glanced at the wall clock. There was one more thing she had to do now. She walked back to the nurses' home and put a small pile of coins beside the phone, then dialled Mark's number.

"Mark Laurence."

Mark's voice sounded cool and somehow official.

Jo took a deep breath. "Hello, Mark. It's me."

Mark sounded surprised. "Jo? Where have you been? I rang you at the nurses' home a couple of times, but they said you'd gone home. I didn't have the number. I didn't . . ."

Jo was surprised that she felt so calm, so in control of the situation. "I went home for a couple of days. I had some thinking to do, some decisions to make."

"But you didn't say a word. I had no idea where . . ."

"There was no time," said Jo. "And I needed to think — without distractions."

"But you had no right, going off like that without telling me," said Mark, and Jo felt sure she detected a note of real irritation in Mark's voice. "I mean, there's the weekend in the New Forest. We have to make arrangements." There was a long pause. "You are coming, aren't you, Jo? I'll pick you up Friday evening . . ."

Jo felt calmer by the minute. She fed in another coin and used the delay to take another deep breath. "No, I'm not coming. I told you, Mark, I'm on duty on Friday and Saturday. I can make it later on Saturday, but . . ."

Mark didn't let her finish the sentence. "Saturday's no good! The rest of us are going down on Friday."

"Then you'll have to go without me," said Jo. "I'm on duty, and that's all there is to it. And, Mark, I'm not going to say I'm ill. I'm not prepared to do that — even for a weekend with you."

Mark's voice sounded cold and distant. "I see. So nursing comes first? And where does that leave me?"

"Nursing doesn't come first," said Jo quietly. "I think there's room in my life for my studies and for you. But if you can't accept that . . ."

Mark's voice sounded harder, colder. "I don't know. Maybe I'll ring you after the weekend."

The weekend spent with your friends, just as you'd intended, Jo thought, and felt suddenly chilled. She shivered. The love she'd felt for Mark seemed to be ebbing away fast. It was an almost physical, tangible feeling — love evaporating, disappearing, retreating. Jo felt sure of herself now. "No, I don't think there'd be any point in your doing that, do you?"

Now Mark sounded angry and bitter. "Perhaps not."

"Goodbye, Mark," said Jo.

Mark made no reply, but the phone clicked, and was dead. Jo put down the receiver and leaned heavily against the wall. That's it then, she thought grimly. It's over. Finished. But she didn't feel sad, sorry for herself; the feeling she experienced was overwhelmingly one of relief. At least the decisions were made now, her future decided. So it was to be a future without Mark. Jo remembered Mark's hard, cold voice as he asked where she'd been. He hadn't shown too much understanding, had he? Hadn't expressed any concern for her at all? So Mark's over, she told herself, then spoke out loud: "So what?"

Next stop for Jo was Nigel's ward. She found him sorting old magazines and newspapers from his locker. "What's all this?" she asked.

When Nigel looked up he was grinning from ear to ear. "They're letting me out, Jo. I'm going home at the weekend. Helen's coming for me in her dad's car."

Jo hugged Nigel. "That's brilliant news. Oh, Nigel, I'm so pleased. Goodbye St Stephen's, hello world, eh?"

"Yeah. I feel like I've been a bystander for the last few months, a spectator. Now I want a bit of the action again. And I can't wait to spend time with Helen again. Being here without her has made me realize how much I need her."

"Mmm," said Jo, her smile subsiding suddenly as thoughts of Mark swam into her mind.

"What's wrong?" asked Nigel.

"It's Mark, Mark and me. It's over. Finished."

"Oh, I'm sorry, Jo. Are you really upset about it, or . . ."

Jo shrugged. "I'll get over it, I suppose. I'll have to, won't I? I just feel a bit lost, a bit detached at the moment. Incomplete, somehow."

"Like you've lost a leg or something?"

Jo had to laugh despite herself. She aimed a punch at Nigel's shoulder. "Not quite! Not quite!"

Nigel looked suddenly serious. "Well, I can't say I'm too sorry about Mark, Jo. I never really liked the sound of him. I mean, I know I never met him, but . . . well, I just don't think he was for you."

"Thank you, Claire Rayner, for those words of comfort."

"Sorry. I'm not much good at dishing out advice and things, but maybe Andy . . ."

"Andy?"

"Maybe you should talk to him about it. He seems to be the person you respect most. And I can tell how much he cares about you."

Jo smiled. "You're the second person to say that in as many days."

Nigel thumped a pile of old newspapers on the bed. "Well, think about it," he said. "Just think about it."

CHAPTER FIFTEEN

HAPPINESS

Months later, Jo and Lynn sat side by side in the School of Nursing gym. Rows of chairs filled with learners faced a long table where the head of the school and the nurse tutors sat facing them.

"It's a bit like those American college graduation day ceremonies you see in films," whispered Jo to Lynn.

Lynn nodded. "Sssh. Listen."

The senior nurse tutor was reading out a list of the names of learners who'd passed their third year exams and were now fully qualified Registered General Nurses. When Andy's name was read out Jo had to resist a wild urge to clap and whistle, but made do with a beaming smile instead. As everyone clapped after the last name had been read out, she spoke to Lynn, though her eyes were firmly fixed on Andy, who was carefully studying his hard-earned certificate. "I'm so proud of him," she said. "Andy

Callaghan, RGN. Sounds good, doesn't it."

"So will Jo Carr, RGN, in time. And Lynn Brooking, RGN – I hope."

"Well, at least we've got through the first year. And you got best marks, as I seem to remember, even though you have spent most of your off-duty time with Rob."

Lynn spoke out of the corner of her mouth. "I guess I'm just brilliant, that's all."

After the awards ceremony there was a wine and cheese reception. Jo and Lynn stood together looking at the learners and nurses who filled the room. Some had become good friends in the past year.

"Who would have thought things would have worked out like this?" said Jo, scanning the crowd for one particular face.

"Yes. Do you remember our first day here?"

"How could I forget it?" said Jo. "I thought you were going to be a real drag."

"And I think I was a bit scared of you. You seemed so confident, and I felt so unsure of myself."

"You didn't show it! Remember that row we had?"

Lynn nodded and they both laughed happily.

Jo was the first to recover. "Seriously, I'm really glad we shared. You were great when I was so miserable after I split with Mark, coming out with me when I knew full well you'd rather be with Rob."

"Isn't that what friends are for? Anyway, Rob understood. I'm so lucky to have found him, Jo, I really am. He's been good for me."

"Yep. I think he peeled away the mousey outer covering and let the real Lynn step out."

"You make me sound like an onion."

Jo pondered that one. "No, I was thinking more of a banana!"

"Charming!"

"Anyway, I knew things between you and Rob would work out. It was all in the stars."

"Oh, no, not horoscopes again," said Lynn. "Go on, tell me all about it."

"Well, remember the first time I ever read out your horoscope — you didn't even know what star sign you were?"

"I remember the occasion vaguely — but I don't remember what the horoscope said."

"It said something like — white is a very significant colour for you. White will be of great importance in your love life."

"But I don't get it. Rob's name isn't White."

"No," said Jo. "But think of a white bird."

"A dove? A duck?"

"No, stupid. A swan! Swans are white, aren't they? And Rob's name is Swann. See? It was all written in the stars."

Lynn groaned loudly.

"And there's something else. White, think about it. Rob wears a white coat, doesn't he?"

Lynn groaned again. "I think you should take over from Russell Grant on the television."

Jo didn't answer, but took a newspaper clipping from her pocket. "Nearly forgot," she said. "I saw this in the *Clarion*. What do you think?"

Lynn read aloud. "Self-contained flat. Suit two. Near hospital. Are you thinking of trying for it?"

"Yes," said Jo. "Why not? We don't have to live in the nurses' home now we're big, grown-up second years. I fancy a place of our own."

"Our own? You mean, you and Andy, you're going to . . ."

"No, idiot. I mean us, you and me. What do you think? Shall we try it?"

"I hadn't really thought about leaving the home, but — yes, why not?"

Just then Jo noticed a familiar face scanning the crowd of bobbing, chatting heads. "Andy!" she called. "Over here!"

Andy fought his way through the crowd. "Let me look at you," said Jo. "I want to see if you've changed."

Andy laughed. "Why should I have changed? I've only got my registration, I've not grown a new head or anything."

"But I'm so proud of you, I could burst," said Jo. "Andy Callaghan, RGN. It sounds so good."

Lynn decided to leave Jo and Andy alone. "See you later," she said. "I'm going to see if I can find Nishma. I expect she'll be at the buffet table."

"See you," said Jo and Andy together.

They looked deep into each other's eyes, big grins on their faces. "Happy?" said Andy.

"You bet," said Jo. "Here, take this," she said, handing Andy her half-empty wine glass and paper plate.

"Why? Where are you going?"

"Nowhere," said Jo. "I just want to hug you, and I can't do that with my arms full, can I?"

"Hold on. I've got a better idea," said Andy, cramming the glasses and plates onto an already-full table nearby. He took Jo's hand and pulled her through the crowd into the corridor outside. It was suddenly quiet after the babble of voices.

"Now you can hug me," he said, and Jo stretched up her arms, her eyes scanning Andy's face. She stroked his cheek with her fingertip.

"I think I love you, Andy Callaghan, RGN."

"I love you, too. And I know it."

Andy's arms encircled Jo and pulled her close. Their lips met in a long, relaxed kiss that made Jo forget everything but that moment. It felt so good, so right. In Andy's arms was the only place she wanted to be.

When their lips parted again Andy still held Jo close, nose to nose. Then Jo pulled away slightly. Her look was thoughtful and a little pensive suddenly. "What is it?" asked Andy.

"Well, it's just something I should have asked you before now."

Andy looked puzzled. "Ask away."

Jo laughed, hugged Andy close again, and whispered in his ear. "I've just never asked you what star sign you are. I mean, we may not be compatible . . ."

"Forget star signs and horoscopes," said Andy. "Take it from me — we're just made for each other!"